PREACHING
THE
NEW COMMON
LECTIONARY

PREACHING
THE
NEW COMMON LECTIONARY

YEAR B
Revised and Enlarged Edition
Advent, Christmas,
Epiphany

Commentary by:

Fred B. Craddock
John H. Hayes
Carl R. Holladay

ABINGDON PRESS
Nashville

Preaching the New Common Lectionary
Year B   Advent, Christmas, Epiphany

Copyright © 1984 by Abingdon Press
Revised and enlarged edition copyright © 1987 by Abingdon Press
Fourth printing 1990

This book is printed on acid-free paper.

Library of Congress Cataloging in Publication Data

CRADDOCK, FRED B.
    Preaching the new common lectionary. Year B,
Advent, Christmas, Epiphany.
    Includes index.
    1. Bible—Homiletical use. 2. Bible—Liturgical
lessons, English. I. Hayes, John Haralson, 1934– II.
Holladay, Carl R. III. Title.
BS534.5.C7   1987   251   87-15290

ISBN 0-687-33855-7

(pbk.: alk. paper)

(Previously published under ISBN 0-687-33845-X)

MANUFACTURED IN THE UNITED STATES OF AMERICA

Contents

Epiphany

Special Days

Introduction

It might be helpful to the reader if we make a few remarks about our understanding of our task and what we have sought to accomplish in this volume. The following comments will touch on four topics.

The Scripture in Preaching

There is no substitute for direct exposure to the biblical text, both for the preacher in preparation and for the listener in worship. The Scriptures are therefore not only studied privately but read aloud as an act of worship in and of itself and not solely as prelude to a sermon. The sermon is an interpretation of Scripture in the sense that the preacher seeks to bring the text forward into the present in order to effect a new hearing of the Word. In this sense the text has its future and its fulfillment in preaching. In fact, the Bible itself is the record of the continual rehearing and reinterpreting of its own traditions in new settings and for new generations of believers. New settings and new circumstances are properly as well as inescapably integral to a hearing of God's Word in and through the text. Whatever else may be said to characterize God's Word, it is always appropriate to the hearers. But the desire to be immediately relevant should not abbreviate study of the text or divorce the sermon from the biblical tradition. Such sermons are orphaned, released without memory into the world. It is the task of the preacher and teacher to see that the principle of fidelity to Scripture is not abandoned in the life and worship of the church. The endeavor to understand a text in its historical, literary, and theological contexts does create, to be sure, a sense of distance between the Bible and the congregation. The preacher may grow impatient during this period of feeling a long way from a sermon. But this time of study can be most fruitful. By holding text and parishioners apart for a while, the preacher can hear each more clearly and exegete each more honestly. Then, when the two intersect in the sermon, neither the text nor the congregation is consumed by the other. Because the Bible is an ancient book, it invites the preacher back into its world in order to understand; because the Bible is the church's Scripture, it moves forward into our world and addresses us here and now.

The Lectionary and Preaching

Ever increasing numbers of preachers are using a lectionary as a guide for preaching and worship. The intent of lectionaries is to provide for the church over a given period of time (usually three years) large units of Scripture arranged according to the seasons of the Christian year and selected because they carry the central message of the Bible. Lectionaries are not designed to limit one's message or restrict the freedom of the pulpit. On the contrary, churches that use a lectionary usually hear more Scripture in worship than those that do not. And ministers who preach from the lectionary find themselves stretched into areas of the canon into which they would not have gone had they kept to the path of personal preference. Other values of the lectionary are well known: the readings provide a common ground for discussions in ministerial peer groups; family worship can more easily join public worship through shared readings; ministers and worship committees can work with common biblical texts to prepare services that have movement and integrity; and the lectionary encourages more disciplined study and advance preparation. All these and other values are increased if the different churches share a common lectionary. A common lectionary could conceivably generate a community-wide Christian conversation.

This Book and Preaching

This volume is not designed as a substitute for work with the biblical text; on the contrary, its intent is to encourage such work. Neither is it our desire to relieve the preacher of regular visits to concordances, lexicons, and commentaries; rather it is our hope that the comments on the texts here will be sufficiently germinal to give direction and purpose to those visits to major reference works. Our commentaries are efforts to be faithful to the text and to begin moving the text toward the pulpit. There are no sermons as such here, nor could there be. No one can preach long distance. Only the one who preaches can do an exegesis of the listeners and mix into sermon preparation enough local soil so as to effect an indigenous hearing of the Word. But we hope we have contributed to that end. The reader will also notice that, while each of us has been aware of the other readings for each service, there has been no attempt to offer a collaborated commentary on all texts or a homogenized interpretation that belies our own areas of specialized knowledge. It is assumed that the season of the year, the needs of the listeners, the preacher's own abilities, as well as the overall unity of the message of the Scriptures will prompt the preacher to find among the four readings the word for the day. Sometimes the four texts will join arm in arm, sometimes they will debate with one another, sometimes one will lead while the others follow, albeit at times reluctantly. Such is the wealth of the biblical witness.

A final word about our comments. The lections from the Psalter have been treated in the same manner as the other readings even though some Protestant churches often omit the reading of the psalm or replace it with a hymn. We have chosen to regard the psalm as an equal among the texts, primarily for three reasons. First, there is growing interest in the use of Psalms in public worship, and comments about them may help make that use more informed. Second, the

Psalms were a major source for worship and preaching in the early church and they continue to inspire and inform Christian witness today. And third, comments on the Psalms may make this volume helpful to Roman Catholic preachers who have maintained the long tradition of using the Psalms in Christian services.

This Season and Preaching

This book deals with the Seasons of Advent, Christmas, and Epiphany. It is our hope that this three-in-one format will not lure the preacher into moving through these services with a kind of sameness of spirit that fails to acknowledge and embrace the various changes in the seasons of the spirit. For observing Advent, which begins the Christian year, we have biblical texts that speak of promise, preparation, hope, and anticipation. Those who preach on these texts will want to capture their moods of restrained excitement. Christmas differs from Advent as fulfillment differs from expectation, as today differs from both yesterday and tomorrow. Having is an experience quite different from hoping, for hoping moves the spirit down the road of reflection, asking, Now what? Then comes Epiphany, the celebration of the manifestation of Christ to the nations. Themes and images of light, revelation, and public proclamation abound in these texts. Nothing is subdued or veiled here; "This is my beloved Son" is the word from heaven. Advent's whisper in Bethlehem is now a shout in the streets of every city. Good preaching will not only say the words but will also attempt to carry the tune.

Fred B. Craddock (Gospels)
John H. Hayes (Old Testament and Psalms)
Carl R. Holladay (Epistles)

First Sunday of Advent

Isaiah 63:16–64:8; Psalm 80:1-7; I Corinthians 1:3-9;
Mark 13:32-37

On this first Sunday of Advent the church is called to longing for God's redeeming presence, to the sorrow that is not sentiment but repentance, and to expectation. Both Isaiah and the psalmist lead in a lament by the believing community and a prayer for God to come in saving power. Mark offers a description of how it will be, and is, when God's Christ comes to perform God's final work of judgment and redemption. In the epistle, Paul reminds even a troubled church as Corinth that God's coming in Christ is the formative act for the Christian community.

Isaiah 63:16–64:8

The limits of this particular reading have been set by the confessional reference to the fatherhood of God in the opening and closing verses. As part of a communal lament, this passage constitutes a powerful plea for God to intervene in history in a decisive fashion to bring redemption to his people. As a special petition for divine redemption, the passage embodies the central themes of the Advent Season—the sense of a need for redemption, the feeling of unworthiness before God, a longing for God to act, and the assurance that as Father God is also Redeemer.

Two background issues should be noted about this text, one historical and the other literary. First of all, the historical context of the pericope should be noted. The passage belongs to a part of the Book of Isaiah (chapters 56–66) which had its origin among the Jewish exiles in Babylon after the fall of Jerusalem in 587 B.C. The people, here praying for redemption, were alienated from their homeland, living among

13

foreigners, and saw themselves as suffering for their sins and estranged from God.

In the second place, Isaiah 63:16–64:8 is one component in a larger literary unit, namely, a lament offered by or on behalf of the community (for similar communal laments, see Pss. 44; 74; 79). The larger unit begins in 63:7 and ends in 64:12. A lament is a prayer to God for help in time of need. As such, laments contain a description of the trouble or distress of the worshiper as well as a plea for God to redeem the one praying from the destitute condition that produced the turmoil and the anxiety.

Isaiah 63:16–64:8 contains the description of the distress situation along with the plea for redemption. In the text, there is a movement from the description of distress to the plea for redemption and then a return to the situation of distress. These two components are introduced and concluded by a statement of confidence in God who is addressed as Father. Thus we have the following outline in the pericope: an introductory statement of confidence (63:16), a description of the distress (63:17-19), a plea for God's redeeming activity (64:1-4), a second description of the distress (64:5-7), and a concluding statement of confidence (64:8).

Let us first examine how the text talks about the distress. In the initial description of distress (63:17-19) the focus is on the people's alienation and estrangement from, and their loss of contact with, God. Three aspects of this condition are emphasized. (1) In verse 17, the community declares that it is God himself who makes them err and sin and who hardens their hearts so that they do not fear the divine. Old Testament faith was quite willing to claim what makes moderns cringe; namely, that God could bring evil upon his own people and harden their hearts so that punishment was inevitable (see Isa. 6:9-13, 45:7; Deut. 32:39). (Honesty in our proclamation should prevent us from toning down such an emphasis since frequently our misery seems or feels God-sent and the deity appears as our enemy!) (2) The temple, representing God's presence, has been destroyed and adversaries occupy God's holy place (verse 18). Foreigners are in the place where God's people made contact with the divine. (3) Verse 19 declares that the sense of alienation from God is so great that it is as if God had never been their ruler and they had never borne and confessed his name. They feel as if they had never belonged to God.

The second description of distress focuses on the sinful state of the people and their sense of absolute lostness. Numerous metaphors are used to describe such a condition. They feel unclean and thus ostracized from normal life (see the condition of the leper in Lev. 13:46) or like a polluted garment, contaminated, fit only to be destroyed. Like a withered leaf or wind-blown trash, the people find that their iniquities have destroyed the substance of life (verse 6). The human condition is so bad that no one anymore seems faithful—they live, not in God's hand, but in the clutches of their iniquities (verse 7).

The petition for redemption (64:1-4) pleads for God to act, not in some normal way, but with decisive force as he did before when he caused mountains to quake and fire to blaze forth (see Exod. 19:16-18; Ps. 114:3-6). Isaiah 64:4 concludes the plea for divine intervention with a statement of confidence— God can so act for those who wait since neither ear nor eye knows of any God so great!

The opening and concluding statements of confidence affirm the people's trust in God whom they call Father. To be able to address God as Father is a claim to be his children in spite of all the evidence. The people may feel as if they cannot claim the patriarchs, Abraham and Israel, as their father (63:16) and that they are merely clay (64:8), yet it is faith in God as Father that supplies a confidence transcending any other relationship that is the ultimate basis of their hope.

Advent, like Isaiah 63:16–64:8, is concerned with human alienation from God and with the drastic consequences of human sinfulness, but like this text, it looks beyond these to God's intervention from heaven (64:1) in the incarnation when the alienation is transcended and human sinfulness is overcome.

Psalm 80:1-7

Like Isaiah 63:16–64:8, Psalm 80 is a communal lament. Such prayers were frequently offered by the community in the context of a national fast after some calamity had threatened its existence or dissipated its life. On such occasions, the people broke with the normal routine of life, assembled at sanctuaries, offered sacrifice, lamented their distress, and entreated the deity to intervene on their behalf.

The first seven verses of this psalm have been selected for Advent reading because of the material's description of distress and the plea for restoration. These verses ought to be studied and understood in light of the entire psalm, or else they will appear as only a truncated part of the whole. The integral relationship of the entire psalm, which is addressed to the Deity, is substantiated by the threefold repetition of the refrain in verses 3, 7, 19, which is almost identical in all three. Perhaps in the service of communal lamentation, these refrains represent the part of the liturgy spoken by the entire congregation while the rest of the psalm was voiced by the priest or person in charge.

An outline of the entire psalm makes for a better understanding of the opening verses. The following are the component parts: (a) address to the Deity with an initial plea (verses 1-2), (b) the initial refrain (verse 3), (c) a description of the distress (verses 4-6), (d) the second refrain (verse 7), (e) a second description of the distress (verses 8-13), (f) a plea for God's help (verses 14-17), (g) a vow or promise of loyalty to the divine if salvation is forthcoming, and (h) the concluding refrain.

Two primary images of the Deity appear in the psalm. At the beginning God is addressed as the Shepherd of Israel (verse 1), a very common way of speaking of the deity in the ancient Near East where sheep raising and the importance of shepherds were widely understood. In verses 8-13, God is portrayed as the viticulturist or vineyard keeper. Both images imply a God who must oversee the items under his supervision with great care, concern, and tenderness.

Now let us focus more closely on the verses of today's lection. The opening address to the Deity would suggest that the psalm originated in the Northern Kingdom of Israel. The use of the name Joseph for the people as well as the reference to the northern tribes of Benjamin, Ephraim, and Manasseh (the last two were names of the sons of Joseph; see Gen. 48:1) point in this direction. Also the reference to God as "thou who art enthroned upon the cherubim" was a divine epithet used of God's sitting enthroned upon the ark which contained cherub decorations. (Cherubs were considered semidivine figures probably depicted with an animal body, human head, and bird wings; in the ancient world, they were not depicted as fat little winged angels!). This epithet was used at the old ark shrine in Shiloh (see I Sam. 4:4). All of this implies that the distressful situation requiring a lament had to do with a calamity involving the northern state of Israel. What the calamity was is unknown, perhaps defeat in some military campaign.

In the description of the distress the people complain that God is angry with their prayers, that is, unresponsive to their pleas for help (verse 4). Unlike a good shepherd who provides his flock with sustaining food and good water, God is depicted as feeding them with bread of tears and giving them tears to drink in full measure. That is, God is accused of bringing misery and suffering on them and failing to function as a good shepherd (verse 5). Instead of protecting them from their enemies, God becomes their enemy. Their plight is so bad that their neighbors make fun of them and their adversaries hold them up to ridicule (verse 6). It is, indeed, the dark side of the divine which the people have experienced. Just as they see that their hope is in God so they attribute their misery to the same source.

The refrain in verse 7 is an appeal for God to help; if only his face would shine forth, that is, if the divine disposition would change, then the people would be saved.

Just as Israel gave thought and expression in this psalm to its need for God's help and saw its situation as desperate without divine aid, so we in the Advent Season think of the misery of human existence and look forward to the shining of God's face in the coming of the Redeemer. Advent, like Israel's lamentation services, should be a time to ponder the conditions of life under the anger of the divine and life's futility without the presence of God's shining face.

I Corinthians 1:3-9

This passage embodies two of the formal features with which Paul typically opens his letters: the greeting and prayer. Since the letter was written to be read aloud to the congregation assembled as a house-church, probably in the home of Gaius (cf. Rom. 16:23), both elements were appropriate for a worship setting, the one as a congregational greeting, the other as an opening prayer. As one would expect, the prayer was crafted to fit the special needs of the hearers as they awaited their founding apostle's advice and instructions contained in the letter that was to follow.

The invocation of grace and peace combines the standard forms of greeting commonly used by Gentiles and Jews, but here they have become thoroughly Christianized. They are in no sense ordinary greetings. The source of both grace and peace are seen to be in God the Father and the Lord Jesus Christ.

The opening prayer of thanksgiving can be profitably compared with similar prayers in Paul's other letters (cf. Rom. 1:8-17; Phil. 1:3-11; I Thess. 1:2–3:3; II Thess. 1:3-12; also II Cor. 1:3-7). Such prayers normally have two functions: to set the mood and overall tone of the letter that follows and to serve as a "table of contents" by telegraphing in advance some of the main concerns to be unfolded in the letter.

The tone of the opening prayer is one of confidence and reassurance. Paul begins by recalling the decisive event in which all Christian experience is anchored: God's gracious gift of Christ. It was this that provided the fundamental reference point for all future orientation and the basis on which Paul provided further instruction and exhortation. This in itself is instructive, for it shows us how Paul the pastor anchored his teaching and instruction in that which his readers had already received and experienced (cf. I Cor. 15:1-11).

Paul reassures his readers that they are rich in speech and knowledge, that they are not deficient in any spiritual gift, and finally that the commitment which they began as Christians will be sustained through the assistance of God until the day of Christ. As is well known, each of these becomes a major theme which is developed later in the letter (cf. 8:1-3; 13:1-13; 15:1-58).

As the remainder of the letter makes clear, a situation had developed within the church that caused some of the members to become painfully aware of their deficiencies. Some of the weaker members, probably newer converts, were being intimidated by some of the stronger, more experienced members who claimed greater and more impressive spiritual accomplishments. As a result, some of the members were anxious about their own status before God and apparently confused about the coming of Christ. Consequently, much of the letter is written to strengthen the whole church collectively. On the one hand, Paul insists that the better side of "knowledge" is love (8:1-3), and that every member, regardless of the gifts one has received, is a vital member of the body (chapter 12).

Given this level of anxiety and uncertainty—not at all uncommon for newer Christians—Paul's stress on the fidelity of God is well directed. "God is faithful," he asserts, reminding them that the God who had called them into the fellowship with Christ could, and would, sustain them until the end. That God can be trusted unconditionally is reiterated later in the letter (I Cor. 10:13) and is frequently asserted by Paul (cf. II Cor. 1:18; I Thess. 5:24; II Thess. 3:3; cf. Heb. 10:23; 11:11; I John 1:9; Rev. 1:5), although it is the one axiom of Christian faith consistently called into question by many of life's experiences.

The strong eschatological emphasis in the passage, seen especially as the prayer moves to a conclusion, can be profitably explored during Advent. It is worth noting that there was considerable confusion within the Corinthian church concerning the last days and that this elicited from Paul his most extensive set of systematic comments about the resurrection (chapter 15). Moreover, eschatological misunderstandings had ethical implications. The belief that some had already experienced the second resurrection led to spiritual arrogance and resulted in open immorality. Accordingly, Paul's remarks here serve as a reminder that the resurrection is still future and that the interim need not be spent in anxiety. Instead, Christians may live in full confidence that God is faithful and that God can sustain to the end those who have committed themselves to the life of faith and trust. Even the least gifted can live in the assurance that the God who calls also sustains.

Mark 13:32-37

"And what I say to you I say to all: Watch." It may be disconcerting at first that the Gospel lection to begin Advent is from Mark who has no birth narrative and that the particular reading from Mark is from a discourse about the end of time. But the appropriateness not immediately apparent becomes clear upon reflection. Advent, after all, has to do with the coming of the Lord, the birth being but one form of the appearance of Christ. And at the center of faith's understanding of the end time is the coming of the Lord. Because God is "The One Who Comes" to strengthen, to reveal, and to redeem, the posture of the people of God is always the same: expectation and hope.

Mark 13:32-37 is the conclusion to a lengthy discourse of Jesus sometimes called "the little Apocalypse" because of its similarity to the Apocalypse in John. Upon leaving the temple in Jerusalem for the last time before his death, Jesus made the pronouncement that the temple would be destroyed: "There will not be left here one stone upon another" (verse 2). The speech itself is in response to questions posed privately by Peter, James, John, and Andrew (verses 3-4). Scholars have long recognized the composite nature of the discourse, as evidenced by portions of it being found in other contexts in Matthew and Luke. For example, the statement that no one except God knows the time of the end (verse 32) is a pronouncement found in many places and in a variety of forms (Matt. 24:42; 25:13; Luke 12:38, 40; Acts 1:7). Because this verse contains its own truth it can as easily conclude the preceding paragraph (verses 28-31) as it can begin our reading for today. In fact, without verse 32, verses 33-37 constitute a literary unit which begins and ends with the same word and contains one governing thought. Apparently the author who drew together these sayings into one speech wanted the emphasis to fall here.

The final word of Jesus prior to the passion story is a thrice-repeated word (verses 33, 35, 37): "Watch."

Because of the instructional and hortatory nature of Mark 13, many have surmised that it was a portion of a catechism for new converts. But whether to new Christians or to those who already bear the burden of discipleship, these words are definitely addressed to believers who not only suffer but who must also try to interpret events that seem to contradict the expectations of those who trust in God. At the time Mark wrote his Gospel, Jerusalem and the temple lay in ruins. Civil strife had outlived Roman patience and the threats begun by Emperor Caligula (A.D. 39–40) are now (A.D. 70) carried out. What did this disaster mean for the purposes and promises of God? Jewish prophets had fed the war effort with messianic ideology, but how were followers of Jesus to understand the end of the holy city and the temple? Added to the persecution at the hands of religious and political authorities and the anguish of families torn apart by differing loyalties (verses 9-13) was the unbearable confusion created by false messiahs and false prophets (verses 6, 22). False messiahs were claiming, "This is the Second Advent; I am Christ returned," and false prophets were turning religion into an almanac: "The signs are right; this is the end." Experiencing most heavily now the absence of Jesus, the faithful are torn between giving themselves up to despair or reaching for any flicker of hope.

To that church and to all the faithful everywhere ("And what I say to you I say to all") the word of our text is both encouraging and demanding. The believers are not robbed of their expectation of a final day, a day of relief and vindication. That time will come, but it will be at God's determination and accompanied by signs God will give. All human calculations are confusing and futile. In fact, the day of the Lord is not to be tied to any political condition or religious institution. The weals and woes of any nation, even a nation claiming to have a central place in the purposes of God, do not dictate the time or place or form of God's advent. Nor do religious institutions, even those established to serve and honor God such as temple or church, fix the calendar of heaven. God survives all human structures and institutions, sometimes having to shatter and re-create the communities that exist for God's work in the world. In other words, true hope is trust in the faithfulness of God, constant amid the rise and fall of the worst and the best of human achievement.

The clear evidence of trust in the faithfulness of God is faithfulness in our work and witness. This is the meaning of being alert and watchful. To watch is not to scan the heavens, read the horoscope, comb through obscure texts, and begin every sentence with the words, "When the Messiah comes." Such uninvolved waiting for the Messiah is not hope; it is postponement and evasion. Looking upon scenes of human misery and mouthing, "When the Messiah comes," has nothing to do with this text. The brief parable in verses 34-35 (conflating themes from parables in Matt. 25:14 ff. and Luke 12:35 ff.) makes it quite clear what life is for the disciples of Jesus. It is as though a master, absent on a journey, had left his servants in charge, *each with work to be done,* with a keeper at the door. To watch is to be faithful in our work, as though we were already in the presence of the One for whose coming our hearts are anxious.

Second Sunday of Advent

Isaiah 40:1-11; Psalm 85:8-13; II Peter 3:8-15a;
Mark 1:1-8

Today's readings shift the mood from lament and longing to the good news of God's coming soon. Both Isaiah 40 and II Peter 3 remind us of conditions in the world that persuade some that salvation is nowhere near. But those same texts boldly make their announcements of comfort and redemption to waiting believers. Mark uses Isaiah 40 to say the promise is being fulfilled in the appearance of John the Baptist to prepare the way. Psalm 85 helps us enjoy now the anticipated consequences of God's presence.

Isaiah 40:1-11

This passage opens what has been called the prophecy of Second Isaiah. Isaiah 40–55 is generally traced back to a single anonymous prophet who carried out his work in the exile just as the Persian ruler Cyrus had begun his conquest of the Babylonian Empire (see Isa. 44:28; 45:1). Isaiah 56–66, or at least parts of this material, may have come from the same unknown prophetic spokesperson.

In its wars with the Babylonians, Judah had been overwhelmingly defeated. Its capital city, Jerusalem, had been captured in 597 B.C. and King Jehoiachin and his family taken into captivity in the first Babylonian deportation of exiles (II Kings 24:1-17). Ten years later, Judah was again locked in battle with the Babylonians. This time, in 587 B.C., Jerusalem was destroyed, its walls pulled down, the temple burned, the Davidic family removed from the throne, and additional Judeans deported. The crisis which these events created for the Jewish community is echoed in the Book of

Lamentations which speaks of the horrible calamities that befell the city. Second Isaiah's message should be read in parallel columns with the Book of Lamentations because the misery and destitution that Lamentations bemoans, Second Isaiah proclaims are coming to an end and salvation is at hand.

The burden of Second Isaiah's preaching was twofold. On the one hand, he had to convince the despondent exiles that events in the international scene, especially the meteoric rise of Cyrus, was the work of Yahweh, Israel's God—that God was again moving in history and had not deserted the world or the chosen people. On the other hand, the prophet had to convince his own people that Cyrus' conquest would bring a new day for the exiles and the Judeans—that God had forgiven the people and was going to inaugurate an act of salvation that would free them from exilic conditions.

Isaiah 40:1-11, the introduction to the remainder of chapters 40–55, has many of the features of a prophetic call to prophesy (see Isa. 6; Ezek. 3). In this text, however, the focus is not on the one who is to be the messenger but instead on the message itself.

Four voices are depicted as speaking in this text: in verses 1-2 the prophet reports what he hears God saying; in verses 3-5 another voice other than God speaks; in verses 6-8 still another unidentified voice makes proclamation; and, finally, in verses 9-11, apparently the prophet issues his clarion call for Judah to carry the Good News, "the gospel," of God's coming to the cities of Judah. The best way of getting into this text is to examine the content of the four speeches associated with the four voices.

In the divine speech, God commands, first of all, that comfort be proclaimed to the people. The term translated comfort is a plural imperative and suggests that "comfort" is what is to be proclaimed by the subsequent three voices. Now it is God who, with a note of urgency, declares that comfort and tenderness are the message of the hour. Unlike the earlier Old Testament lessons for Advent in which the people lament, cry, and plead to God, the emphasis in this text falls on the initiative of God who demands that the people be addressed. In the second place, the proclaimed comfort is based on the divine decision that the people have suffered enough, the years of disciplinary judgment are over, the price for the sins of the past has been paid. Note the threefold divine affirmation: warfare (or the compulsory time of service) is ended, iniquity is pardoned, God's demand for punishment for sin has been met because the people's suffering and affliction have paid double (or perhaps "the equivalent") for all their sins. The end of strife and the forgiveness of sin herald a new relationship.

The second voice (of an angelic messenger?) calls for the preparation of a highway in the desert, a highway for God whose glory shall be revealed publicly (40:3-5). The imagery of such a highway probably harks back to the fact that in Babylonian religion, special processional ways were constructed along which the images of the gods were carried in an annual procession so the people could see the representations of the objects of their worship. Yahweh's highway was to lead (from Babylon) across the desert (back to the Land of Promise). Just as in the first exodus that led the people through the desert with all its troubles and heartaches so now Second Isaiah has a messenger announce a second exodus in which nature is to be transformed and an unobstructed way for God is to be prepared.

The third voice proclaims the assurance of God's word which, unlike the fleeting, fading, withering, and temporary, is proclaimed as standing forever. It is the word that is the basis of hope and certitude. It is the divine word proclaimed from the time of creation and throughout history (Isa. 40:21) that now is addressed in a new form so that the people can look forward to the "new thing" that God promises (Isa. 43:18-19) certain that the word is secure for "the mouth of the Lord has spoken" (verse 5).

Finally, the prophet calls on Jerusalem to serve as herald, as the evangelist, of God's coming (verses 9-11). Two factors are stressed about the coming of the divine. On the one hand, God comes with might and strength to rule, yet, on the other hand, God comes with great tenderness as the shepherd who gathers the lambs, cuddling them in the bosom, and watching carefully over the yet unborn.

Psalm 85:8-13

The verses in this psalm have been selected as part of the Advent cycle because they speak of some of the consequences of God's promised salvation. The proclamation of verses 8-13, however, is best seen in light of the psalm as a whole. Verses 1-3 recall an earlier time when God had restored the fortunes of the people, forgiving their sins, and withdrawing the divine wrath. What this section talks about specifically remains uncertain. Does it refer to the return from exile proclaimed in glorious terms in Second Isaiah? Or does it revolve around features of Israel's great autumn festival season when God was annually proclaimed as forgiving the people's sin on the day of atonement and proclaiming for the people a new slate and a new fate for the coming year? Probably the latter should be seen as the context of this psalm's usage and the phenomenon described in verses 1-3. The prayer for God to revive and restore the people in verses 4-7 would thus be a plea that God would again, in the festival, put away his indignation and anger and display instead his salvation and thus revive the people.

The lectionary text, according to the above interpretation, would be an oracle spoken in the service of worship by some cultic official (priest? prophet?) who already envisioned and anticipated what God's response would be and what consequences it would produce. (Note that verses 1-7 are addressed to the deity and are thus prayers while verses 8-13 speak about the deity somewhat similar to the preaching and proclamation of a prophet.)

Psalm 85:8-13, like Advent, anticipates the coming and already perceives its consequences. What God will speak is peace (*shalom!*). The consequences of Yahweh's speaking are described in a play on a number of terms—faithfulness, righteousness, peace, steadfast love. What these terms describe are all good qualities. They are depicted coming together as if they were two who meet and kiss or if one springs from the earth and the other looks down from the sky. That is, because God speaks, full harmony and unity result. Here, ideal qualities are merged.

Verse 12 returns to more mundane matters; God will give what is good and the land will yield its increase. This again suggests the use of this psalm in the fall festival when the old agricultural year ends and a new year begins. In Palestine, the rainy season, from October through April, is followed by a rainless season, from May through September. Thus the new agricultural year in the Bible began after the first rains in the fall when new crops could be sown. The fall festival was celebrated as the hinge between the ending of the old and the beginning of the new. Thus the oracle of verses 8-13 closes with the promise of a good agricultural year. (Perhaps, verses 4-7 suggest that the previous year's harvest had not been good.)

Advent, like the fall festival season in ancient Israel, is the hinge that joins the old and the new. Anchored in the past with all its failures, shortcomings, sufferings, and heartaches, it nonetheless is attached to the future and already joined in anticipation to the time when God "will speak peace to his people" (verse 8).

II Peter 3:8-15*a*

This passage exhibits a twofold structure: instruction about the Parousia (verses 8-10) and moral exhortation (verses 11-15*a*). It arises in response to "scoffers" (3:3) who find the notion of Christ's Second Coming incredible. From their perspective, they find no pattern of divine intervention in history. They have seen an earlier generation of Christian apostles and leaders, the "fathers" (verse 4), die before experiencing Christ's return. Living now in a later generation, they are disillusioned at the prospect that Christ will ever return. They are convinced that things now are pretty much as they always were and are likely to continue along the same course. The source of their views is not clear, but such skepticism is known to have existed among various religious groups in the ancient world.

The author of Second Peter perceives the problem as not only shortsightedness but as essentially a matter of whether one's world view is broad enough to admit divine activity within the human arena. If God can play a decisive role in the beginning of things, so is it possible to see the end of history from a similar perspective (verses 5-7).

The scoffers are reminded not to assume that God calculates time as they do: "With the Lord one day is as a thousand years, and a thousand years as one day" (verse 8). God does not necessarily follow a human calendar. Moreover, they should reckon with the possibility that God has delayed as a means of extending mercy and forbearance to humanity. After all, God's ultimate desire for humanity is that no one should perish but should respond penitently to the divine will. The final reminder is that however overdue the day of the Lord may seem to be, it will be unexpected, coming "like a thief" (verse 10). The language used to describe the final consummation reflects a Jewish apocalyptic outlook: "The heavens will pass away with a loud noise, and the elements will be dissolved with fire." The notion that the world would end in a final conflagration was not uncommon in antiquity. Though the sentiments expressed are couched in ancient terms, they are frighteningly modern for those who have attempted to visualize the prospects of a nuclear holocaust.

However difficult it may be for Christians to conceptualize Christ's Second Coming—and its cruder depictions certainly strike many modern believers as naïve—the fact remains that it is now possible to conceive of the instantaneous dissolution of all human life in a way heretofore unimaginable. Such thoughts always have a sobering effect.

The second part of the passage quite understandably turns to moral exhortation. In early Christian teaching, eschatological instruction was intimately connected with moral exhortation. As Christians contemplated the end of things, they were enjoined to reflect on their own style of life and conform themselves to the sobering realization that life is moving toward a purpose. Given the possibility of ultimate destruction of all human life as we know it, "what sort of persons ought you to be in lives of holiness and godliness!" (verse 11). The Christian hope is that beyond human depravity there is the promise of "new heavens and a new earth in which righteousness dwells." Accordingly, Christians are urged to practice the moral life, while regarding the

Lord's willingness to delay not as a failure to be punctual but as a generous and merciful gesture toward humanity: "Count the forbearance of our Lord as salvation."

This text is filled with themes rich in possibility for the Advent Season. Many modern Christians find the notion of Christ's Second Coming difficult to comprehend. Rather than recasting this ancient article of Christian faith into terms suitable for a modern outlook, modern believers sometimes respond by abandoning any belief in God as the Omega. The method of approach in the text is itself instructive, for the author anchors his response in theological reflection. He appeals to the Christian doctrine of creation as the basis for a viable eschatology. It is also instructive that he insists on the connection between eschatology and ethics. Abandoning any real conviction about God's ultimate purpose in history all too easily translates into moral laxity, or cynicism about whether there is any ultimate justice. The homiletical task here is to shape a responsible eschatology for modern believers which, on the one hand, preserves a meaningful sense of the future, but on the other hand neither forecloses God's role in that future nor relaxes our responsibility in facing it.

Mark 1:1-8

The Advent Season has no more appropriate voice than that of John the baptizer (Mark 1:4; Mark identifies John by function rather than by title, the Baptist, as in Matt. 3:1). John was a prophet both of anticipation and of preparation, the twin themes for beginning Advent. Our Gospel lesson today introduces John from the earliest and briefest of the four accounts.

"The beginning of the gospel of Jesus Christ, the Son of God" (Mark 1:1). With these words Mark does not simply launch the story of Jesus but provides a title for his narrative. As far as we know this is the first use of "gospel" to refer to a written account of the narrative about Jesus Christ. By referring to his account as "the beginning," the author may have been thinking of a Christian Genesis, but more likely he meant to say that the life, death, and resurrection of Jesus were, for all their central importance, but the beginning of the mission to bear the Good News to every nation under heaven.

And where does one begin a story entitled "The Beginning of the gospel"? In a sense, the beginning is with the prophets of Israel. Most likely the early church had a collection of passages from the Hebrew Bible for use in Christian preaching. Two such texts happily joined were Malachi 3:1 and Isaiah 40:3, both of which announce God's coming, preceded by a messenger to prepare the way. Mark, perhaps because Isaiah 40 is the dominant passage, refers to both as being from Isaiah, a confusion cleared up by Matthew (3:3) and Luke (3:4) by omitting the citation from Malachi. The importance of Malachi 3:1 for Mark is that it identifies the messenger preparing the way as Elijah (Mal. 4:5) and the early church identified Elijah as John heralding the coming of the Lord. Mark also interprets Isaiah 40:3 so that "in the wilderness" locates the messenger (the voice in the wilderness) and not, as in the original oracle, the place of God's appearing (prepare in the wilderness the way of the Lord). By so reading his sources Mark says the prophets bear witness to this "beginning." Here we can see how the Bible understands itself. While the coming of Christ is a new thing God is doing, it is not without a past. John's preaching is news, good news, but it has a history, a memory. Memory is the soil in which hope survives, and that which is remembered is the promise of a faithful God.

In a more immediate sense, however, "the beginning" points not to the prophets but to John himself. It is John who bursts upon the scene creating new excitement, stirring hearts, and gathering all Judea and Jerusalem to the Jordan River, to hear his message of repentance, confess their sins, and receive baptism and forgiveness of sin. John is the beginning of the Gospel for it is his dynamic ministry that prepares the people for the one mightier than he (verse 7). His popularity and influence made an impact upon political (Mark 6:17-29) and religious (John 1:19-28) leaders as well as the common people. How account for it? The curious came, of course, for he was an unusual man, and the nostalgic, too, for this image of Elijah (II Kings 1:8) must have stirred longing for the good old days. But basic to the power of his ministry were the two themes of his preaching: the Messiah is at the door and repentance is essential as preparation to receive him. In other words, he gave his listeners hope and he gave them a way to enter into that hope.

But if we listen to John, "the beginning" is not the prophets or himself but Jesus Christ. Jesus is the Messiah, the Son of God; John is the voice, the messenger, the preparer of the way. Jesus will baptize with the Holy Spirit; John baptizes in water in an anticipatory rite of repentance and forgiveness. Whatever John's followers claimed for him, Mark and the early church are clear in their understanding: John is the forerunner; Jesus is the Messiah. The issue is settled: Jesus Christ is "the beginning."

But the prophets, John and Jesus are but names, figures of the past, unless there is "the beginning" in the effective sense in the lives of those who heard. John's Good News of forgiveness and the approach of the Messiah was not without demand and judgment. Most scholars agree that Matthew 3:7-12 and Luke 3:7-18 preserve original elements of John's message: an ax laid at the root of trees; baptism with fire; the winnowing fork blowing away chaff for burning. And it is to the people of God that this call for repentance comes! The very sermon that God's people had been preaching to the pagan world—repentance and submission to rites of cleansing—is addressed instead to them. Repent of the arrogant assumption that you alone are favored, that you are exempt from the moral demands put on others, that being better than your worst neighbors is your salvation, as though God grades on the curve. Repent, be honest, come clean, unload fruitless patterns of behavior, abandon clever devices for maintaining the illusion of innocence. What could be better news than this: an offer to repent, to confess, to enter into a rite of cleansing, to be forgiven.

Advent pilgrims on the way to the manger must pass through the desert where John is preaching.

Third Sunday of Advent

Isaiah 61:1-4, 8-11; Luke 1:46b-55; I Thessalonians 5:16-24;
John 1:6-8, 19-28

Understandably, the idea and image of the Lord's coming produces both fear and joy. Our texts today assure the faithful to be full of joy. Such is Paul's word to the church at Thessalonica, while both Isaiah and Luke (the Magnificat of Mary serves as the psalm for today) announce good news to the poor, the lowly, and the oppressed. The Gospel reading focuses again on John the Baptist, but this time as witness to the light and life offered to all in Jesus Christ.

Isaiah 61:1-4, 8-11

In analyzing many biblical texts, it is frequently essential to notice any changes in who the speaker is and who are those being addressed. Such a shift in speaker and addressee occurs throughout Isaiah 61. It opens with a confessional statement about God (verses 1-4), then God presumably speaks (verses 5-9), and finally apparently the community communicates (verses 10-11). Nothing is provided in any of the speeches to suggest who the intended audience is. Presumably one should think of the community of the prophet's day as the addressee. In our analysis, we shall divide the text of the lection into the following units: verses 1-4, 8-9, 10-11.

In verses 1-4, a figure speaks about an endowment for a task, the objectives of the task, and the consequences of the task. The entire content of this section is very similar to the so-called Suffering Servant poems found earlier in Isaiah (42:1-4; 49:1-6; 50:4-9; 52:13–53:12). These poems speak about a particular figure assigned to a task which involved not only special functions but also severe suffering. The early church, which interpreted much of the Old Testament as predictions both about Jesus and the life of the church, was certain that these poems were prophecies and that Jesus was the Suffering Servant. Modern scholarship, doubtful that an ancient prophecy about Jesus would have meant much to a generation that lived hundreds of years before his birth, has attempted to identify the figure with someone known to the prophet's audience. Was it the prophet himself? Israel? the exiled Judean king? the Judean exiles? Cyrus? Research has raised numerous candidates for the figure but produced no agreement or certainty on the issue.

Likewise, in this text, one cannot be certain of the mold in which the figure's identity has been cast. Part of the description of the endowment, especially the anointing, suggests a royal figure because in ancient Israel to speak of the anointed (the Messiah) was to speak of the king (see I Sam. 24:6). On the other hand, high priests were anointed in later times and one text speaks of the anointing of a prophet (I Kings 19:16). Thus, the figure may have been conceived in royal, priestly, or prophetic terms or some combination of the three.

The task of the figure incorporates multiple activities. One theme, however, runs through all the descriptions: the work of the figure is to bring a reversal of fate to those in various states of destitution and deprivation. Those to be the recipients of the work of the spirit-filled anointed one are: the afflicted, the brokenhearted, the captives, those bound in prison, and the mourners. As in the earlier Old Testament lessons for Advent, the imagery of the text suggests groups in desperate straits bewailing their conditions and yearning for release. The new note in this text is the assertion that God has now appointed a figure to take action that will relieve the situation primarily in the proclamation of good tidings and good news.

Much of the content of the anointed figure's proclamation is depicted in political rather than spiritual terms. One is reminded of Moses' activity in proclaiming liberation to the Hebrew slaves in Egypt. (a) Good tidings to the afflicted and the binding of the brokenhearted can only refer to the alleviation of these conditions. (b) Liberty to the captives and the opening of the prisons suggest a political act and has led many to think that the figure of the Persian Cyrus may have colored this presentation since he freed many who had been exiled in foreign lands by the Assyrians and Babylonians. Frequently new kings proclaimed amnesty to those enslaved and imprisoned. (c) The reference to the year of the Lord's favor is best understood as a reference to either the coming of a sabbatical year or the year of Jubilee. In the former, the sabbatical (or seventh) year was a time when slaves were freed and debts were canceled (see Exod. 21:1-11; Deut. 15:12-18). The Jubilee, the fiftieth year in a cycle, was the time when slaves were freed, debts canceled, and the landholdings redistributed to their original owners (see Lev. 25). At any rate, both were years of God's favor when human misfortune was reversed and a new beginning proclaimed and realized. For those who benefited, either was a year of release but to those who had subjected others, it was a day of divine vengeance.

Those mourning in Zion would possess new symbols of their status replacing the old symbols: flower garlands rather than ashes, oil to soothe the skin rather than mourning, mantles to wear rather than a fainting spirit (verse 3). The consequences for those blessed would be a new status; they would be a new planting for a new day. In turn, the new status would bring a new task: the rebuilding of the cities and the restoration of the ruins to remove the results of years of devastation (verse 4).

In verses 8-9, God declares his love of justice and his dislike of the opposite and promises the renewal of the covenant, the reestablishment of the proper relationship between the people and the deity. This new status of the people—restored and blessed in a newly built land—would give them respect and thus grant them the opposite of their former status which had made them the laughingstock of their enemies (see Ps. 80:6).

In the final unit, verses 10-11, the speaker is again difficult to determine. It may be the anointed figure of verses 1-4 or perhaps even the community speaking as an "I." At any rate, one can see the pattern indicated in the text. The anointed figure proclaims his task (verses 1-4), God responds to affirm the divine activity of covenant reestablishment, that is, the return to a time like the days of old (verses 8-9), and finally there is the enthusiastic assurance expressed by the recipients (verses 10-11) who already see themselves as partaking of the salvation of the new age. Two things should be noted about the description of the new conditions. First of all, newness is expressed in terms of clothing—garments of salvation, robe of righteousness, and wedding attire. The new inner state manifests itself in the outer person. Second, the newness of righteousness and praise springs forth like new vegetation growing among the nations; it is only the beginning but at least a beginning.

Luke 1:46*b*-55

The psalm for this third Sunday of Advent is a song of praise to God who remembers the poor and lowly and delivers them from the proud and oppressive. This psalm is not found among the songs of David but is the song of Mary, mother of Jesus. When the angel announced to Mary that she would bear the Christ Child, she was told that her kinswoman Elizabeth, barren and advanced in years, was now in her sixth month of pregnancy (1:36). So Mary went to the hill country of Judea to the home of Elizabeth and Zechariah, and after greetings were exchanged Mary burst into song.

It is important first of all to note that the song is Mary's not Elizabeth's, as one would expect. The Magnificat is based largely on the song of Hannah in I Samuel 2. The story of Hannah and Elkanah, parents of Samuel (I Sam. 1-2), should be reviewed in preparation for understanding Luke 1:46*b*-55. Hannah, distressed that she was barren, tarried in the temple after a festival, weeping and praying for a child. The priest Eli thought she was drunk. She made known her prayer, promising that if God gave her a son she would give the child to God. Her prayer was answered and she named the child Samuel. When she brought the child to the temple as a gift to God, she sang a Magnificat. The story so parallels that of Elizabeth and Zechariah that one would expect Elizabeth to sing as did Hannah. Both women were older; Hannah was assured of a child while she was at the temple just as Zechariah was; both sons, Samuel in the one case and John in the other, were given to God under special vows and they lived as set apart for God. A few late manuscripts are so attracted to the similarities between the two families that they have replaced Mary's name with that of Elizabeth in Luke 1:46. But that "And Mary said" is the reliable reading is very well established. But it does not fit for a young virgin to sing Hannah's song. The tradition of God granting a son to elderly childless couples is well established: Abraham and Sarah were given Isaac, Manoah and wife were given Samson, and Elkanah and Hannah, Samuel. In that tradition of God blessing the barren, John now comes and to that history he belongs. But when a song from that tradition is sung by a young virgin, the tradition is interrupted, the old is new and the familiar is strange. God is doing a new thing. Had Elizabeth sung Hannah's song, it would have been said that God continues to be gracious to the barren, as of old. But when the virgin Mary sings, it must be said that God's grace is not as of old, but new and strange and surprising and beyond understanding. This child will not be as Isaac or Samson or Samuel, but will be the Son of God.

And what is it that Mary sings? Her song opens with joy and praise that God has favored a handmaiden of low estate. But only briefly does she speak of herself. She sees God's grace and goodness toward her as but a single instance of the way of God in the world. God blesses the poor and oppressed and hungry and in the final eschatological reversal, God will bring down the proud and rich oppressors and exalt those who have been disfranchised, disregarded, and dismissed. The most remarkable quality of the song is that the justice God will bring to pass is spoken of in the past tense: has shown strength, has scattered the proud, has put down the mighty, has exalted the lowly, has filled the hungry, and has sent the rich away empty. Why the past tense? According to the latest news reports these things have not yet occurred.

Of course, these conditions are not yet, but one of the ways the faithful express trust in God is to speak of the future with such confidence that it is described as already here. Such faith is prerequisite to being a participant in efforts to achieve that future. To celebrate the future as a memory, to praise God for having already done what lies before us to do: this is the way of the people of God. Without this song of praise, the noblest efforts to effect justice in society become arrogant projects, messianic moves by one group against another, competing for camera time. God's people parade before they march, for history teaches us that without the parade, the march may soon become lockstep, and perhaps even goosestep. Who, then, will remain to say, "My soul magnifies the Lord"?

I Thessalonians 5:16-24

Though addressed to the young Thessalonian church, this concluding series of exhortations is broadly applicable to all Christians. Previously, Paul has given pithy words of advice directed at the internal life of the community (verses 12-15). He now turns his attention to the inner life of Christians, enjoining them to "rejoice always, pray constantly, and give thanks in all circumstances" (verses 16-18). Though general in scope, each of these injunctions has special force in light of his previous discussion where he addresses the anxieties within the church arising from their misunderstandings about the Parousia (4:13–5:11). Such anxiety could all too easily produce grief and gloom (4:13). The confidence that God had destined the saints not for wrath but for salvation (5:9) should come as a source of encouragement and serve as a basis for edification and hope. Therefore, "rejoice always" is not an empty cliche here.

Similarly, vigilance in prayer is appropriate behavior for the Christian who lives with an eye to the future committed to God. Giving "thanks in all circumstances" may have struck the Thessalonians as odd advice, considering the affliction they had endured (1:6; 2:14-16). Yet, because of their steadfast hope (1:3), they had reason to live in gratitude, not for their affliction per se, but for the confidence which enabled them to rely on a promise-keeping God: "He who calls you is faithful, and he will do it" (verse 24). Just as Paul could appeal to the fidelity of God in opening his letters (cf. I Cor. 1:9), so did he find it an appropriate note on which to conclude this letter.

The Thessalonians are enjoined not to extinguish the fire of the Spirit (verse 19). Endowments of the Spirit historically have been unsettling and unpredictable: "The [Spirit] blows where it wills" (John 3:8). Yet, this prophetic energy within the church is essential for renewal. One response by the church is to "despise prophesying." Paul cautions his readers not to squelch the prophetic voices within their midst. Rather, he calls them to be discriminating. "Test everything," he urges, insisting that they be discerning as they listen to the voices of prophecy among them. The following words may be general moral exhortation, but more likely are to be understood in this context of prophetic discrimination: "Sift out what is good, and steer clear of what is evil." Christians are urged not to be naïve in listening to those who claim to speak in behalf of God. They should recognize that prophetic words should be weighed rather than accepted blindly.

For the church living in the interim between the "already" and the "not yet," Paul's advice here retains its force. One way of preparing for Christ's coming is to resign oneself to fate, lapse into passivity, and suspend all judgment. Later, Paul addresses this tendency to adopt a stance of quiet resignation (II Thess. 3:6-13). Yet, Paul never allows such a stance to be a responsible option for the Christian who lives with the expectation of Christ's return. Accordingly, the church's role, even as it faces the "not yet," is one of confident hope, balanced with vigilance in prayer and thanksgiving, as well as the exercise of an active role in discharging its prophetic ministry. Taken seriously, Paul's advice here keeps us from adopting an attitude of disengagement as the church faces the realities of life and the world even as it looks to Christ's coming.

The final section of the passage is a prayer calling for the God of peace to bring about the full sanctification of communal and individual Christian life. Indeed, every fabric of the human personality—"spirit, soul, and body"—is committed to the care of God who prepares the church for the Parousia.

John 1:6-8, 19-28

Because the psalm for this Third Sunday of Advent is the Magnificat (Luke 1:46b-55), many preachers will no doubt be attracted to that reading as basic to the sermon for the day. This may be further motivated by the fact that the Gospel lection focuses on John the Baptist who was the subject of last Sunday's Gospel (Mark 1:1-8). Attraction to the rich and beautiful Magnificat is understandable, but John 1:6-8, 19-28 certainly should not be slighted as though its message were repetitious; it definitely is not.

All four Evangelists give attention to John the Baptist, seeking to achieve a balance between the praise appropriate to his role in relation to Christ and a polemic against the movement in John's name which grew alongside the church and in a sense competed with it. According to Acts 18:24-28, a preacher from Alexandria knew only the baptism of John, and in the city of Ephesus Paul began his mission among a group of disciples who had received John's baptism (Acts 19:1-7). Even today, a small sect in Iraq called Mandeans trace their history back to John the Baptist. No wonder, then, that the Gospels try to keep John in the role of forerunner to Jesus and only in that role recognize his greatness. Mark deals with John by being brief, citing John's acknowledgment that Jesus is "mightier than I," and contrasting their two baptisms. Matthew says that while John baptized Jesus he was hesitant to do so, saying he should be baptized by Jesus (3:13-15). Luke, who interweaves the stories of the births of John and Jesus, says that when Mary entered the house of Elizabeth, John leaped in Elizabeth's womb in recognition of the mother of the Lord (1:39-45).

In today's Gospel text, the Baptist is presented twice: in the Evangelist's word about John (1:6-8) and in John's word about himself (1:19-28). The first presentation is as a prose insertion into the poetry of the Prologue. The Prologue (1:1-18) is in praise of the eternal divine Word, agent of creation and redemption, who becomes flesh in Jesus of Nazareth. But twice (verses 6-8, 15) the author interrupts the poem to explain quite emphatically: I am not talking about John. While it is true he was sent from God, he was not the

Word, he was not the light, he was not the life of the world. John was a witness to the Word, Jesus Christ. Three times in verses 6-8 and again in verse 15 John is called "a witness." That simple word best captures this Gospel's portrait of John.

Following the prologue, the narrative begins with what amounts to a title for the account which continues through verse 24: "And this is the testimony [witness] of John" (verse 19). John's witness consists of two parts, the one concerning himself (1:19-28) and the other concerning Jesus (1:29-42). John's testimony concerning himself was not a part of his proclamation but in response to investigators, priests, and Levites, sent from the Jews and from the Pharisees in particular (verse 24). When asked, "Who are you?" notice how strongly stated is the reply; he confessed, he did not deny, he confessed he was not the Christ. The implication is that some people believed that he was. John claimed no title or station; in his own estimation he was not the Christ, or Elijah, or any other prophetic forerunner of the Christ. He was, he said, a voice (verse 23). When asked why he baptized, he made no claim for his baptism, neither as a means of forgiveness nor of reception of the Holy Spirit. What others claim for what one does and what one claims for oneself are often different, and properly so. John's identity, says this Gospel, was totally in relation to Jesus Christ to whom he was a witness. Even as John spoke, Jesus stood among them as one they did not know (verse 26).

Even though John came prior to Christ, as a witness he is in many ways a model for all who follow. "You shall be my witnesses" (Acts 1:8). Witnessing is most difficult, not because we do not believe but because we do. The more important the subject matter the harder it is to say the words. Speech stumbles over feelings of inadequacy and unworthiness; the words proceed cautiously to the listener's ear for fear of offending. Glib talkers who are "really good at it" seldom persuade us that they have just come from the empty tomb. And the church corporately is called to witness. During Advent how full the church calendar is; it can be such a rich and rewarding experience. But over it all, over every song, cantata, party, gift, service of worship, act of charity, let the church first say, "We are not the light but came to bear witness to the light." The true Light is in the world, but among the people he is often One they do not know. Some miss him perhaps because they have made looking for the Messiah a way of life, preferring their own desires as to what life will be when the Messiah comes to the responsibilities that follow the confession, "The Messiah has come and it is Jesus." The first great task of a messiah is to bring to an end the search for a messiah.

Even in Advent we witness to the One who already stands among us, who has already come.

Fourth Sunday of Advent

II Samuel 7:8-16; Psalm 89:1-4, 19-24; Romans 16:25-27;
Luke 1:26-38

Today's readings are, appropriately enough, celebrative and doxological. The narrative base is provided by II Samuel 7 which tells of God's covenant with the house of David, and Psalm 89 celebrates that covenant while calling on God not to forget. God did not forget, says Luke, but remembers and sends Gabriel to tell Mary that through her the promise will be kept. Paul reflects on what that fulfilled promise of God means for Israel and for all the world and closes his Roman letter in a burst of praise.

II Samuel 7:8-16

The seventh chapter of Second Samuel contains the fullest narrative account of the Davidic covenant. The Old Testament lection comprises only a portion of the chapter, namely the part that focuses specifically on the promises of God to David.

In the narrative of Second Samuel, David has finally acquired "rest from all his enemies round about" (7:1) and decides that it is time to build a house (a temple) for Yahweh whose ark, the symbol of the divine presence, was residing in a tent in Jerusalem (6:17). With the help of the Phoenician king, Hiram of Tyre, David constructed a great palace of cedar in the capital city (5:11; 7:1). The king felt that such difference in life-style—he in a cedar palace and the ark in a tent—was hardly commensurate with the way affairs should be.

David proposed building God a "house" and this theme forms the backdrop for the subsequent promises of God to the king. The narrator plays on the double meaning of house,

42

signifying both temple, in the case of God, and dynasty, in the case of David. The king's plan was submitted to the prophet Nathan who first approved the temple construction but then withdrew approval after a nighttime consultation with God (7:2-7).

With God's disapproval of the construction of a temple, the focus shifts from God's house to David's house and from David's desires to the divine promises. (According to Ps. 132:1-5, David had sworn that he would never enter his house nor sleep until he had found a dwelling place for God, but there is no reference to this promise of David in the books of Samuel.) Several features are noteworthy in Yahweh's promises to David.

1. David is reminded of his humble origins as a shepherd from which he was elevated to become prince over Israel (verse 8). Here one finds a common motif of the Bible: God's sympathy for the powerless and benevolence for the humble. Another way of describing this motif is to see it as the Cinderella theme—the success of the unpromising. Over and over again this theme reappears in Scripture (see II Sam. 2:7-8; Ps. 113:5-9). One can recall the aged Abraham and Sarah without child; Moses as a babe afloat on the crocodile-infested Nile; motley unorganized slaves laboring in Egypt; and, as Advent approaches, a Babe in a manger. In all of these, the meek and powerless for whom God has special concern find their ultimate status a reversal of their original status.

2. David is reminded of his conquest over his enemies (see II Sam. 8). He is also reminded that his reputation will be like that of the great ones of the earth and that his name will be remembered forever (verse 9)—a theme that reappears in the emphasis on Jesus' name in the New Testament.

3. David's success and greatness would be shared by his people Israel who would live in tranquillity in their own place (verses 10-11a). The God who is described as constantly wandering (verse 6) promises the people a place where they will be planted, and the humble David, who is elevated, has a people to share the glory of the newly acquired state.

4. Above all, God promises David that his family will be established forever. There is no house for God who dwells in

the temporality of a tent; but for David there is an eternal house! The continuity of David's family and the eternity of its rule is promised in general terms in verse 16 which highlights and summarizes the central promise to David—a dynasty, a kingdom, and a throne, forever. All subsequent Jewish expectations of a coming Messiah were fed in one way or another by this text.

5. Verse 12 focuses on the immediacy of the promise. One of David's immediate offspring will succeed him; his dynasty will not be replaced like that of Saul (verse 15). Here, of course, the narrator and reader anticipate Solomon who would come after David and build God a house (verse 13).

6. Finally, David's son will also be God's son: "I will be his father, and he shall be my son" (verse 14). The ancient Israelites probably did not think of David's son as actually being "sired" by God, that is, in terms of physical descendancy but in terms of a relationship. David's son and God would be like Father and son. Sonship in this text, however, involves not so much special privilege as the promise of God's chastisement of the son for disobedience. Here the narrator anticipates the eventual lack of complete obedience on Solomon's part and the subsequent disruption of the kingdom at his death (see I Kings 11).

Second Samuel 7:8-16 thus forms the *locus classicus* for the expectation of the eternal rulership of the house of David and is the fountainhead for all messianic hopes about the revival of David's rule after the fall of Jerusalem in 587 B.C. As part of the readings for the Advent Season, it looks forward to him who is the David to come.

Psalm 89:1-4, 19-24

This psalm offers the fullest exposition of the divine covenant with David and the promises it involves that can be found anywhere in the Old Testament (see verses 19-37). In some respects, II Samuel 7 may be seen as merely a narrative adaptation of the Davidic promises celebrated in this poetic form in the royal cult of the Jerusalem court.

Psalm 89 is in reality a lament which speaks of the divine promises to David after they have all been called into question. The conclusion of the psalm, verses 38-51, bemoans the humiliation of the Davidic ruler who is the object of divine wrath, whose covenant is renounced, whose strongholds are in ruin, and for whom all the promises of God seem to have failed. The description of the king's condition simply piles up one disappointing condition upon another. The psalm ends with a complaint about the loss of God's love and faithfulness and a prayer for God to note how the king bears in his bosom the insults of the nations roundabout and how the enemies mock the footsteps of the anointed (the Messiah).

If one takes this material as reflective of some actual historical situation, then the king must have suffered a severe humiliation in battle. In fact, the psalm sounds as if it is a description of the consequences that resulted from the destruction of Jerusalem by the Babylonians.

But this week's psalm lection does not focus on the humiliation aspects of the psalm; it focuses on the positive. Verses 1-4 both remind and praise God for divine faithfulness and steadfast love which are always the basis for confidence. Note that God is reminded that steadfast love is forever and his faithfulness as sure as the heaven. (Although the minister may not wish to highlight the point, these are exactly the divine qualities called into question in verse 49. Perhaps few psalms so stress the twofold quality of the deity—the divine care and the divine forsakenness as this psalm.) God is made to recall that he swore to David that his descendants would rule forever and his throne endure for generations. The ancient Hebrews were not bashful when it came to reminding God of the divine commitments and to reiterating the promises on which they banked their hopes. (One should remember that when this psalm was read or used in public worship, the person who spoke the first four verses with their calm serenity and secure promises was aware of the trauma yet to be expressed before the Psalter scroll was rolled together and neatly tied and tucked away again.)

Verses 19-24 focus on portions of God's eternal promises to David and recall the words in God's vision in which David was chosen and exalted among his people (see II Sam. 7). Several factors about David and God's relationship to him are stressed, and it must be recalled that the David spoken of here is more the idealized David of messianic quality than the David of history. (1) David was found by God (see I Sam. 16:1-4). Here the emphasis is placed on the divine initiative. The true servant is the one whom God separates out, not the one who grasps at equality or the one who strives for superiority. He who would claim to be the messiah should always be questioned. (2) As the anointed, David is set apart, set aloof from the rest, where he, like the New Testament Messiah, must know what it means to be one "apart." (3) David is promised that victory over his enemies and dominance over his foes are part of the assurance granted since it is God who stands behind him and strikes down his opponents and foes. The interpreter here must remember that ancient Israelite life was always threatened and that survival could never be taken for granted. While this emphasis on being constantly threatened might sound a bit paranoid, even Jesus is said to have struggled with Satan in the wilderness. (4) Finally, the psalmist quotes God as promising that faithfulness and love for David are certain and that in God's strength David's horn will be exalted—that is, his status will be secure.

This psalm, like Advent, calls on people to rely on the divine promises even when those promises seem to lie shattered at the feet of those who pray, but who pray for the coming redemption in spite of the realities within which they live.

Romans 16:25-27

This doxology is traditionally attributed to Paul but its place in the manuscript tradition is disputed. In some manuscripts, it is located at the end of chapter 14, and in at least one manuscript it is omitted altogether. Not only is the style more involved than Paul's, but the central theme of the mystery, once hidden but now revealed, is more reminiscent of the later Paulines.

The gospel as a mystery, formerly hidden but now revealed, is not prominent in the undisputed Pauline letters, but not however absent (cf. I Cor. 2:6-10; cf. I Cor. 15:51;

Rom. 11:25). It is much more fully developed in the deutero-Paulines (Col. 1:24-29; 2:2-3; Eph. 3:1-13). Although the content of the mystery could focus on the Christ-event as the central feature, in its later formulation it also encompassed the work of Christ as it made possible the inclusion of the Gentiles within the messianic community. It is especially this latter emphasis that becomes more fully articulated in Colossians and Ephesians. Indeed, this appears to be the case here, especially if verse 26*b* is rendered literally, "to bring about the obedience of faith" for all the Gentiles.

Embodied within this doxology is what appears to have been a well-established type of early Christian preaching. This form of proclamation had as its central focus what had been present, though hidden, since eternity, but had finally been revealed in Christ. This early Christian homiletical practice is instructive, and might well suggest a point of departure for appropriating the text now. As an Advent text, this passage reflects the shift that occurs in the lectionary in the Advent Season, where there is a gradual shift from the Lord's promised coming to the Lord's first coming. This theme of that which has been hidden as now being revealed dovetails especially well with the Johannine prologue in the lectionary of the third Sunday of Advent, and is a natural sequel. It might profitably be explored as a continuation of the Johannine passage, although theological reflection is taking place in a different mode.

It should also be noted that the emphasis on the prophetic writings (verse 26) anticipates the reading of the Old Testament text from Isaiah on Christmas Day. The universality of this revelation as embodied in the inclusion of the Gentiles also provides expositional possibilities.

The doxology especially highlights the strengthening capacity of the gospel and the preaching about Jesus Christ. The clear sense of the opening words is that Christian readers who begin to realize more fully the cosmic scope of God's revelation in Christ can only stand in awe. Reaching as it does from eternity to eternity, God's divinely revealed mystery encompasses the whole of human history. It is this that no doubt caused this pattern of preaching to excite early Christians. Accordingly, the structure of the doxology itself reflects this same sense of breathtaking awe, for it stops in midair and concludes with the only natural response—confessing God as "the only wise God" to whom eternal glory through Jesus Christ is given.

At Advent, in particular, is this sense of wonder elicited as one approaches the moment in the church calendar when the disclosure of God in human form again occupies center stage.

Luke 1:26-38

For the preacher who had planned to fuss at the congregation about Christmas commercialism or scold the once-a-year worshipers, it is too late. The angel Gabriel is already here with a startling announcement and the news is totally disarming.

Angels were not a part of Jewish theology in its earlier stages, apparently entering late as an influence from Persian religions in which angels abounded. In some circles angels were given special assignments as guards or messengers or caretakers, and certain ones had names, such as Michael or Gabriel. Coming out of late Judaism, Christianity was from the start influenced by the widespread belief in angels and demons. And so Luke tells us that the angel Gabriel came twice from God's presence with good news, first to Zechariah to say that he and Elizabeth were to have a child in their old age (1:5-25), and then to Mary to announce that in her virginity she would conceive and bear the child Jesus, son of David and Son of God (1:26-35). The child of Zechariah and Elizabeth would prepare the way for God's coming (1:17), and God's coming would be in the child of Mary conceived of the Holy Spirit (1:35).

Before trying to distill a theme or central message from this text, the preacher would do well to approach the passage in two ways:

First, the literary style and quality of Luke's composition are important for understanding what this text says and does. It is well known that the author of the third Gospel was a conscious literary artist and nowhere is that more evident than in the first two chapters. Many believe here Luke is sharing materials used in the worship of the early church.

Filled with songs, the liturgical character of the entire narrative is evident. Doxological texts deserve doxological sermons. Of the passage before us now, 1:26-38, two qualities should be noted: one, the form of the announcement by the visiting angel, here and to Zechariah (1:5-25) is in the pattern of such stories in the Jewish Scriptures. The angel appears (Gen. 16:7; Judg. 13:3), the person visited reacts (Gen. 17:1-3), the person is reassured (Gen. 17:4ff.), the birth is announced (Gen. 16:11; Judg. 13:3), the one to be born is named (Gen. 16:11), the child's future is predicted (Gen. 16:12; Judg. 13:5), an objection is raised (Gen. 15:8; Judg. 6:15), a final reassurance or sign is given (Gen. 17:21; Judg. 6:17ff.), and the word is accepted (Gen. 16:13; Judg. 6:24).

Second, the entire narrative is filled with the language of the Jewish Scriptures: "Hail, the Lord is with you"; "you shall conceive and bear a son"; "the Holy Spirit will come upon you"; "let it be to me according to your word"; "with God nothing will be impossible." Unlike Matthew who often tags a citation, "As it is written," in order to prove or authorize his point, Luke weaves the language and phrasing of the Scriptures into his own narrative. For example, Matthew quotes in full Isaiah 7:14 to prove the virgin birth was according to prophecy (1:22-23) while Luke merely echoes Isaiah 7:14 with his introductory comment about the angel visiting a virgin named Mary. Luke is no less filled with Scripture than Matthew, but the difference is important for those who communicate the Gospel materials. Matthew argues, establishes, proves; Luke tells a story. Sermons should reflect the difference.

In addition to approaching the text literarily, the passage calls for theological reflection. A visiting angel dazzles us, an obedient Mary moves us, and a virgin birth arouses our minds, but the chief character in the story is God. God is here portrayed as a God of grace and of power. Grace fills the story because God is sending a gift to the world. Gift is the correct word because all the conditions of normal human action and achievement are absent. There would have been room enough for praising God and saying, "This is the Lord's doing," had Mary and Joseph been, like Elizabeth and Zechariah or Sarah and Abraham, old and barren. How

49

much more so since the announcement of the birth of God's Son is to a girl, young, single, and still in her virginity. The cross speaks of grace, to be sure, but so does the manger. And the power of God? In Genesis 18 Abraham and Sarah receive heavenly messengers who promise they shall have a son. To the bewildered old couple the messenger says, "Is anything too hard for the Lord?" (verse 14). To the frightened and bewildered Mary, the angel says, "For with God nothing will be impossible" (Luke 1:37). This is the creed behind all other creeds. The church should recite it often, not only at the manger, not only at the empty tomb, but on any occasion of reflecting on its own life, joy, and hope.

Christmas, First Proper
(Christmas Eve/Christmas Day)

Isaiah 9:2-7; Psalm 96; Titus 2:11-14;
Luke 2:1-20

The waiting is over; the Lord has come. Luke tells the story of the Messiah's birth simply and quietly, reserving angelic announcements and songs for the shepherd's field. Isaiah 9 also sings of the birth of the Messiah, but in the triumphant tones of a coronation. Such also is the mood of Psalm 96, celebrating the eternal reign of God in all creation. The epistle, in a more practical vein, reminds us that our lives are framed between "Christ has come" and "Christ will come."

Isaiah 9:2-7

The use of this text in Handel's *Messiah* has indelibly etched it into the Advent-Christmas Season. Its references to a light amid the darkness, to the birth of a son, to the longing for peace with justice and righteousness are now intertwined with all those other sentiments that we associate with Christmas and with the advent of new hope.

Probably Handel's, and our own, use of this material has taken numerous liberties with the original meaning of the passage. In origin, the text probably had nothing to do with the actual birth of a baby for surely no one would turn over the government to a babe still at its mother's breast. In spite of this, however, just as all great literature can be read and appreciated in a variety of ways, so this text has tended to lose its moorings in earlier history and although not used in the New Testament it has become an integral feature of the Christmas celebration of the Christ story.

One way of viewing this text which is widely accepted by scholars is to understand it as a composition by the prophet Isaiah for use at either the coronation of King Hezekiah or on the anniversary of the king's accession. Hezekiah began to rule in Jerusalem sometime before 720 B.C., although his exact dates are uncertain. Of all the Old Testament kings, other than David and Solomon, only Hezekiah and Josiah were praised as great monarchs (see II Kings 18:5; 23:25). Of Hezekiah, it was said, "He trusted in the Lord the God of Israel; so that there was none like him among all the kings of Judah after him, nor among those who came before him" (II Kings 18:5). Let us, for the moment, see how this text might have once fitted the situation of Hezekiah's coronation.

Verses 2-5 are very much filled with the imagery of battlefields and the sounds of war and yet they open with the affirmation that a light is now shining in darkness and that a time for rejoicing is at hand. Verses 4 and 5 speak of a burden which has been lifted from the people as in the days when the Midianite suppression was lifted from Israel (see Judg. 7:15-25). How does one best understand this portion of the text?

First of all, Assyria the foreign aggressor had conquered most of the Near East after about 750 B.C., bringing Israel and other states to the north under their control. Judah, however, had remained neutral. Prior to 730, Israel, Syria, and other states, but not Judah, sought to break away from Assyrian control. Since Judah, ruled by King Ahaz at the time, refused to go along, Israel and Syria invaded Judah and sought to depose him. The prophet Isaiah, however, encouraged Ahaz to remain true to God and neutral in the struggle (see Isa. 7:1-9). When war broke out and the Assyrians won, the threat of Israel and Syria were broken. Thus the pressure on Judah was relieved. This probably forms the background for the emphasis on good news and the freedom from military pressure in verses 2-5. With the suppression of Israel and Syria, Judah, for a time, was able to live again peacefully in the area. The country may have reaped some benefits from the spoils of war they were not involved in (see verse 3).

Verses 6-7 would have been spoken by Isaiah, not so much about the new political and military situation as about the new king, Hezekiah, who succeeded his father Ahaz

52

sometime shortly before Israel again revolted against Assyria and was finally annihilated (II Kings 18:1, 9).

Verses 6 and 7 seem to reflect clearly aspects of the coronation ritual. The day of the king's accession to the throne was considered the day of his "rebirth" or adoption as the son of God. In Psalm 2:7, the reference to "today" as the day of the king's being begotten is the day of his coronation. Thus as the new son of God (see II Sam. 7:14), the government would be upon his shoulders. As a new son, the king was probably given a new name or set of names or titles. It may have been the function of the court prophet to help name the new children of a king as well as to come up with royal coronation titles. Nathan, for example, gave Solomon the name Jedidiah, "beloved of the Lord" (II Sam. 12:25), and Isaiah had apparently picked out the name Immanuel for a child to be born at the royal court (Isa. 7:14). Verse 6 in the lection seems to refer to four honorific titles given the new king—"Wonderful Counselor, Mighty God, Everlasting Father, Prince of Peace." We know that the ancient Egyptians bestowed such honorific titles on new pharaohs at their coronation. Such titles were expressions of hope and of the new status enjoyed by the royalty. Kings throughout history have borne such honorific epithets—"defender of the poor, preserver of peace, defender of the faith," and others. The late emperor of Ethiopia possessed enough titles to fill a paragraph in a newspaper story!

Verse 7 predicts that the new ruler will enjoy times of prosperity and peace on the throne of David and that he will rule with justice and righteousness throughout his reign. Such prophetic oracles at the king's coronation not only presented the new king with a set of promises but also was a way of reminding the new ruler of his responsibilities.

Although this text probably had a specific setting in ancient Israel—the king's coronation—it is nonetheless messianic through and through and most appropriate for Christmas Day. Just as Jesus is greeted as the Messiah so was the ancient Israel king. Just as the "hopes and fears of all the years" are focused on the new Messiah Jesus, so in ancient Israel, they come to focus on the new monarch whose coronation was the day of his birth as the son of God.

Psalm 96

Psalm 96 is a hymn that calls the people to proclaim the greatness of God in song and praise. Its special appropriateness to the Christmas Season lies in its universal call for all the earth to sing a new song and to worship God.

This psalm probably was used originally in ancient Israel as part of the celebration of the fall festival. One of the aspects of that festival was the celebration of God as creator and king of the world. Evidence suggests that in the festival, it was believed that God re-created or reestablished the earth for the coming year (note verse 10). Though the belief that God re-created the world annually may sound a bit unusual, we must recall that every Christmas is celebrated as the birth of Jesus. So, such repetitions are commonplace in religious expression in worship.

Three emphases in this psalm are noteworthy in addition to its call for the universal praise and worship of Yahweh.

1. Verses 3-6 contrast the Israelite god with those of other peoples. The gods of the peoples are declared to be mere idols, that is, they are human products, impotent and without power (see Isa. 44:9-20). Over against the idols which are the work of human hands is Israel's God who is not only uncreated but is the creator—the One who made the heavens. Thus, in this psalm, the doctrine of creation undergirds the call to honor and praise God. The reference to God's sanctuary in verse 6 may not be a reference to the temple but rather to creation itself which is conceived of as God's sacred place.

2. Just as verses 3-6 emphasize God as creator and thus as unique among the gods, so verses 10-13 emphasize God's kingship and execution of justice. In verse 10, the phrase "the Lord reigns" appears. The Hebrew expression that is translated here could just as easily be rendered "the Lord has become king." Such a translation would indicate that in the fall festival, God annually reassumed the role of king. The basis for God's kingship is found in the fact that "the world is established, it shall never be moved." It is difficult to believe that such an affirmation and its corollary that "God has become king" are based on the original creation of the world

by God. Again the text probably should be seen in its original usage as affirming God's annual reestablishment of the world and its orders. As the one who does this, God thus asserts his divine rulership over the cosmos.

3. A further emphasis in verses 10-13 is God's judgment of the earth. This emphasis too probably reflects an aspect of the fall festival. Just as God reestablishes the world, reassumes the kingship over creation, so also God judges the world. In later rabbinic Judaism, the belief that all the world was judged in conjunction with the fall festival was widely current. We can see this factor already evident in this psalm. Stress falls, however, on the fact that God judges with equity, righteousness, and truth.

Such a psalm as Psalm 96 is very apropos for the Christmas Season since it speaks so much of divine triumph and affirms that a new situation exists in the world. God is king, the world is established, and all that exists in creation—heavens, earth, sea, field, trees, and above all, peoples throughout the world—are called to praise and worship God.

Titus 2:11-14

The pastoral Epistles are noted for their interest in institutional questions and are quite often disparaged because they address overt questions of institutional form and portray stylized modes of conduct. Admittedly, they address concrete ecclesiastical concerns in a way the authentic Letters of Paul do not, but they are not devoid of richly textured theological passages. This text is one such example (cf. also 3:4-7).

This text provides an excellent counterpoint for the traditional Christmas text from Luke's Gospel. For one thing, it is bifocal in its treatment of the Christ-event, linking the two themes of Advent, Christ's first and second coming, into a single piece. In this respect, it sets the Christ-event in a broader theological framework and serves as a reminder that even at Christmas the eschatological dimension of Christ's work is present. The initial manifestation of God's grace through the coming of Christ into the world, while focal in the celebration of Christmas, nevertheless causes us to look forward to "our blessed hope, the appearing of the glory of our great God and Savior Jesus Christ" (verse 13).

The "high Christology" expressed here is also worth noting. This is one of the few instances in the New Testament where Jesus is explicitly referred to as God (cf. Rom. 9:5; John 1:1; Heb. 1:8; also Acts 20:28). In this respect, this passage represents an advanced stage of christological reflection, as does the infancy story in Luke 2:1-20.

Another salutary feature of this text, which echoes Pauline sentiments, but represents a further stage of reflection within the Pauline school, is its emphasis on the ethical implications of the Christ-event. The position of the text within chapter 2 should be noted. The preceding verses contain ethical instructions to various groups: older men (verse 2), older women (verses 3-5), younger men (verses 6-8), and slaves (verses 9-10). Although this version of the "household code" differs from others found in the New Testament (cf. Eph. 5:21–6:9; Col. 3:18–4:1; I Pet. 2:18–3:7), it is nonetheless a clear statement of the Christian imperative. What follows in verses 11-14 is the "indicative" which serves as the basis and motive for the ethical behavior called for earlier. This connection is seen in the introductory word "for," in verse 11.

This is seen especially well within the passage itself, where the educative function of God's grace is unfolded. We are told that the grace of God "trains," or "disciplines," us so that a definable life-style results. At its best, the grace of God disciplines us to renounce "godless ways and worldly desires" (NEB) and evokes "temperance, honesty, and godliness in the present age" (NEB). This is, of course, in keeping with the emphasis in the pastorals on ethical conduct as expressed in more regimented and codified form (cf. II Tim. 2:25; 3:16). While the liberating force of God's grace—the central thrust of Paul's gospel—should not be forgotten, neither should its capacity to shape character be overlooked (cf. II Tim. 1:7; Titus 1:8; I Tim. 2:2).

In this respect, our text merely attests what Christians historically have experienced at Christmas. Reflection on the story of Christ inevitably prompts us to reflect on our own "story," its overall shape and general direction. The work of Christ is properly conceived as redeeming and purifying, yet a chief goal of his redemptive work is to form a people "zealous for good deeds" (verse 14). As earlier theological debates within the early church showed, an overemphasis on good works easily led to a debilitating theology of salvation by good works, and when this was the case, stressing the liberating force of the grace of God was quite appropriate. Our text, however, serves as a reminder that experiencing the grace of God is not simply an existential experience in which the individual achieves freedom from the bondage of the will, but also results in practical acts of Christian charity and good deeds.

Luke 2:1-20

Before looking into the Gospel lesson for today, let us pause a moment to reflect on what it means to preach on Christmas Day. Many ministers find it difficult to preach at Christmas. This is especially true of those in traditions in which the sermon is the centerpiece of Sunday morning, all else serving in satellite roles. At Christmas, however, the sermon and every other element of worship become but a part of the rich tapestry of celebration. Some preachers thus feel minimized and confess an ego problem. Others feel the wealth of the season makes even a good sermon seem poor indeed. Who is capable of rising to an occasion on which the most beautiful texts of the Bible are read, texts that can make our sermons turn pale and stammer? Nor is it uncommon for a minister to be burdened by the heavy pathos that haunts the edge of Christmas. The luxury of the season points up in sharpest relief the conditions of human misery everywhere. Frustrated by the futility of laying a heavy load of guilt on the parishioners Christmas morning, the pastor may prefer delivering a plate of food to delivering a sermon.

Then there are those whose very definition of preaching is exhorting, filling the air with ought, must, and should. Then comes Christmas when the angels and the children combine choirs to go caroling. There is nothing here for the common scold. But most of all, the familiarity of the songs and texts clips the wings of a preacher, sending some in covert searches for something novel, even if it is inappropriate, irrelevant, and has no substance. But the familiar, rather than deadening, can be the preacher's delight. To say the texts and message are familiar is to say they already belong to the listeners, and there is power, enjoyment, and an occasional "amen" when people hear what they already know. This means it is their sermon, not solely the pastor's. Sometimes we need to preach *for* rather than *to* the church. Now to our familiar text, Luke 2:1-20.

Luke's story of Jesus' birth consists of two parts: verses 1-7 give the birth account and verses 8-20 narrate the annunciation to the shepherds. One of the additional lessons provided for Christmas Day by this lectionary is Luke 2:8-20 and so comments on these verses are to be found there. If no other service is planned, one may choose to use that portion of the text in addition to or in lieu of verses 1-7.

Luke 2:1-7 contains three elements: prophecy, history, and symbolism. That prophecy, fulfilled in Jesus, is not a thesis for Luke to establish but is rather a way of telling the story, of weaving old and new together as one fabric. Without referring directly to Micah 5:2, Luke uses all the elements of that prophecy: Bethlehem, house of David, the Davidic Messiah. Similarly Isaiah 1:3 and Jeremiah 14:8 provide the manger and the image of God lodging for the night. No characteristic of Luke-Acts is more pronounced than the author's insistence on the continuity of Judaism and Christianity. The Hebrew and Christian Scriptures tell one story, not two. God is not starting over with Christians, having failed with Jews. What God said to Abraham is coming to pass: In your seed all nations shall be blessed. The story is marked by rejection and resistance, to be sure, but God is faithful to the promise. For Luke, every Gentile believer can properly say, "Abraham and Sarah are my father and mother."

The second element here is secular history. "A decree went out from Caesar Augustus" (verse 1). Historians have had difficulty with Luke's report of the census under Quirinius (verse 2). Has Luke misplaced the census which came later after Archelaus was deposed as ruler of Judea and the country placed under the governor of Syria? The debates fill the commentaries, but regardless of the reliability of Luke's sources, his purpose is clear: to tie sacred to secular history. As God used Cyrus, king of Persia, to effect the divine purpose (Isa. 45), so God uses Caesar Augustus. The coming of Christ is not hidden in a corner; Rome is joined to Bethlehem. The world is God's, and the gospel is for God's world. The Good News does not belong to the church which may decide to share it with the world. Rather, Mary's baby is God's yes to the world, which includes us.

And the third element is symbolism. Why give attention to Jesus as a baby, wrapped, as any baby would be, in swaddling cloths, lying in a manger crib? Why not, like Mark, go straight to his ministry? Luke paints the whole picture in this small scene. God's Son, vulnerable as every infant is vulnerable, subject to all the conditions under which we all live, fully identified with every human being's need for love, lies here unnoticed, without trumpet or drum roll and without a place to lay his head. Jesus lived from crib to cross, but the teller of the story wrote from cross to crib.

Christmas, Second Proper (Additional Lessons for Christmas Day)

Isaiah 62:6-7, 10-12; Psalm 97; Titus 3:4-7; Luke 2:8-20

All the texts for today remind worshipers around a manger that what we are receiving and experiencing is the work of the one God who is, after all, the subject of the entire Bible. It is God who delivers Jerusalem (Isa. 62); it is God who is enthroned over all the earth (Ps. 97); we have received the grace and favor of "God our Savior" (Titus 3); therefore, our song is "Glory to God in the highest" (Luke 2). Those of us who center faith in Jesus Christ need to recall often that Christ came to us, sent from God.

Isaiah 62:6-7, 10-12

The material in this lection has Zion-Jerusalem as its focus, both in its longing for salvation and in the assurance that the city's coming salvation has already been proclaimed and is on its way.

The interpreter of this text and any who would preach on it need to recall that most of the texts in Isaiah 55–66 depict Zion-Jerusalem as still awaiting salvation, a salvation that has been proclaimed but not yet realized.

Who the ancient reader may have thought was speaking in verses 6-7 remains uncertain. The first part of verse 6 sounds like a word of God yet the second part and all of verse 7 seem like the prophet's address. As we have noted with earlier texts from Second Isaiah, this difficulty in determining the speakers is a characteristic feature of the material.

Isaiah 62:6-7 focuses on the work of city watchmen whose task was to warn the population of danger and to proclaim any news or any change of situation. Note what Isaiah 21:6-7 says of their task:

"Go, set a watchman,
   let him announce what he sees.
When he sees riders, horsemen in pairs,
   riders on asses, riders on camels,
let him listen diligently,
   very diligently."

According to Ezekiel 3:16-21; 33:1-9, the watchman was held accountable if the proper warning was not sounded. Here Ezekiel is, of course, comparing the office of prophet to that of watchman and thus highlighting the responsibility of the prophet. Although the watchman's job was important, Psalm 127:1*b* warns, "Unless the Lord watches over the city, the watchman stays awake in vain."

Isaiah 62:6*a* seems to affirm that God has set watchmen over Jerusalem to function day and night. (In ancient Israel, the night was divided into three watches but in later Roman times, four watches were common.) The fact that the watchmen are never to be silent could suggest the constancy of danger or an exaggerated emphasis of their tasks. The second half of verses 6 and 7 assign two unique functions to the watchmen. (1) They are to remind people of the Lord and to keep him in remembrance. This may refer to various blessings spoken by the watchmen particularly if the watchmen were also priests or cultic functionaries (see Ps. 134) who served at night in the temple. (2) A second task of the watchmen is to give God no rest until Jerusalem is established and becomes an object of praise throughout the earth. Such a task for the watchmen certainly sounds abnormal. Those on duty day and night are never to let God find peace until Jerusalem has found peace. Although such statements may strike moderns as impious, the Old Testament here is quite willing to speak of the necessity to keep reminding God of his responsibilities and promises, even to pester the deity (see also Ps. 44:23-26). If the watchmen were priests, then they would be merely representing the people's sentiments to the deity.

Isaiah 62:10-12 shifts the emphasis to focus on preparation for the coming salvation. People are to be prepared, highways cleared of stone, and an ensign set up to mark where the people should congregate. The prophet reiterates what God has already proclaimed, namely, that salvation is coming and that Jerusalem is to receive reward and recompense (see Isa. 40:1-11).

The new status that will come to the people will be reflected in a series of new names: "The holy people," "The redeemed of the Lord," "Sought out," "A city not forsaken" (verse 12). The theme of the different names of the city also appears earlier in Isaiah 62 where the old Jerusalem and the land are called "Forsaken" and "Desolate" (verse 4). The restored city in this same verse will be called "My delight is in her" (Hephzibah) and the land will no longer be called a widow (see Lam. 1:1) but instead will be known as "Married" (Beulah). In ancient Israel such a change of status was frequently embodied in a play on words or a new name reflective of the new conditions (see Hos. 1:4–2:1 and the earlier discussion of Isa. 9:2-7).

In verse 12 of the lection, one finds a variation in the use of plural and single verb forms: "they shall be called" and "you shall be called." If the single "you" refers to Zion-Jerusalem then the plural "they" may refer to foreigners and pagans who seek out the city and thus become part of "The holy people" and "redeemed of the Lord." One of the features of the second half of Isaiah (especially texts in Isa. 56–66) is the conversion of foreigners who turn to Jerusalem and find in the temple "a house of prayer for all peoples" (see Isa. 56:1-8). This could suggest that the foreigners' turning to Jerusalem is also alluded to in verse 14. If so, this makes the text even more appropriate to the Christmas Season, because in the birth of Christ we welcome the universal Savior and, like the Magi, seek out the One whose star lights up the sky.

Psalm 97

Psalms 96, 97, and 98 have been called "Enthronement Songs," since they celebrate God's enthronement and function as king. As we noted in the discussion of Psalm 96, the reenthronement of God was probably celebrated as part of the fall festival. The ceremony in which this was expressed in the cult probably involved the removal from the temple of the ark, the symbol of God's presence. This would have symbolized the temporary "dethronement" of the divine—a parallel to the Good Friday experience. The transference of the ark back into the temple would have symbolized God's reassumption of kingship and his reestablishment in Zion (see Pss. 132; 47).

Psalm 97 opens with the cry, "The Lord reigns," or perhaps better translated, "The Lord [Yahweh] has become king." This affirmation gives expression to the new state of affairs attendant upon God's reassumption of the role of universal king.

This psalm is divided into three stanzas in the Revised Standard Version. Stanza one (verses 1-5) describes, in metaphorical terms, the awesomeness that the Israelites associated with the appearance or theophany of their God (see Exod. 19:16-18). Clouds, darkness, fire, and lightnings suggest that much of the imagery here has been borrowed from phenomena associated with the frequently violent thunderstorms which often occur in the Holy Land. All the imagery in this stanza emphasizes the shattering, abnormal sense of awe that is produced by the presence of the Deity. In spite of the awesomeness of God's presence, the divine throne and thus the divine rule are said, however, to be founded on righteousness and justice and not totally on the display of power.

Stanza two (verses 6-9) stresses the reaction of both pagans and Zion to God's appearance and the manifestation of divine righteousness in the heavens. Both the pagans—idol worshipers—and their gods are forced to bow down and recognize the omnipotence of Israel's God. One, of course, does not have to assume that this actually happened in some historical event. In the cultic worship where this psalm was used, ideal, not actual, conditions were affirmed and hopes, not full realities, were expressed. Zion, on the other hand, can hear of God's appearance and receive the good news with rejoicing for God's judgments are given in favor of Zion. Since Yahweh is exalted above all gods, Zion and the daughters (cities) of Judah can rest in the assurance that they worship the only God who really counts. This uniqueness and righteousness of Yahweh are the basis of Zion's confidence.

Stanza three (verses 10-12) concentrates on God's preservation of those who belong to the people of God. They have nothing to fear. Note the three actions of God emphasized: the Lord loves, preserves, and delivers. The opening line of verse 10 has no hesitancy in declaring that God loves those who hate evil. Ancient Israel had no qualms about affirming hatred if it was hatred of that which God did not condone. The righteous and the upright in heart in verse 11 are probably synonymously used terms. The righteous were those declared in the right in judgment. Since in biblical thought the heart was the center of the will and the intellect, being upright in heart was being consistent in thought and action. (The heart's association with the intellect has been preserved when we say we memorize things "by heart.") Though the psalm closes with a call to rejoice, that is, a call to let human emotions be given free rein, it also closes with a call to worship and give thanks to God.

The use of this psalm during the Christmas Season emphasizes that regardless of how God's appearance comes, in thundering cloud or whimpering babe, only those who worship idols are put to shame (verse 7). Those who belong to God can rejoice and be glad.

Titus 3:4-7

In the earlier text from Titus, it is the "appearing" of "our great God and Savior Jesus Christ" that is central. Here, however, it is the appearing, or dawning (cf. NEB), of the "goodness and loving kindness of God our Savior" that is more prominent. To be sure, the work of "Jesus Christ our Savior" is mentioned later (verse 6), but his incarnation remains implicit within the passage. Strictly speaking, then, the incarnation of Christ is not the major focus of this passage, although it is the set text for the additional Christmas lection.

This, however, might provide an excellent occasion to remind the community of faith of God's role in the incarnation. The New Testament is a pervasively christological book and its main concern, taken as a whole, is to unfold the life and work of Christ and their implications for the life of believers and the believing community. Because early discussion and debate in the first century focused less on the explicitly theological questions, that is, questions about the nature and work of God, many statements about God remain implicit within the New Testament. In fact, it has been suggested that God is the "neglected factor in New Testament theology." Similarly, at Christmas, Christian reflection and preaching about the work of Christ can all too easily overshadow the divine initiative and work of God.

It is striking here that God is called "our Savior," a term we more commonly reserve for Christ, at least in popular parlance. Yet, in the pastoral letters, in particular, God is frequently designated as Savior (cf. I Tim. 1:1; 2:3; 4:10; Titus 1:3; 2:10). It was common practice for Hellenistic rulers to be called "savior," and by the late first century A.D. when our text was written, Roman rulers were receiving, and claiming, the title more frequently and more audaciously. It may well be that the pastorals frequently designate God and Christ as "Savior" in response to the claims made of human rulers in the imperial cult. If this is the context in which these attributions to God and Christ occurred, it is clear how Christians would have forged their faith over against the competing claims of the imperial cult. Here, the issue would have been one of ultimate sovereignty, and the Christian witness is clear, as seen in our text: It is God and Christ who are to be confessed as Savior, not human rulers. The latter are to be respected, indeed obeyed (cf. 3:1), but not worshiped.

Developed in this direction, in the context of Christmas, the text might easily be used to remind Christians that the Christ story invites all persons to look beyond humanly constructed saviors and salvation systems, be they political rulers or systems, national or local ideologies and ideologues, as their ultimate hope.

As the text makes clear, the way of escape from a life of folly, disobedience, various forms of slavery, and internecine behavior begins with the recognition of the "kindness and generosity" of God our Savior. In a once-for-all act, God "saved us" (verse 5) by taking the first bold and dramatic step: He lavishly poured out his mercy through Jesus Christ our Savior (verse 6). The text also asserts that this was done as an act of unprompted and uncalculating mercy, not as an irresistible response to human achievement and progress.

As numerous saving ideologies compete for the attention of modern persons, the Christ story, celebrated throughout the liturgical year but begun at Christmas, still provides a clear option for those attracted to a "life-story" in which acts of unprompted grace, selfless sacrifice, and mercy are the distinguishing traits of its central figure.

Luke 2:8-20

Luke 2:8-20 is the second part of Luke's birth narrative, the first (verses 1-7) having already been discussed as the Gospel lesson for Christmas Eve or Christmas Day. Since verses 8-20 constitute an annunciation, it might be helpful to review the literary pattern common to such stories (cf. comments on Luke 1:26-38, Fourth Sunday of Advent). The annunciation here parallels the angel's visits to Zechariah and to Mary, the three accounts providing the central structure for Luke's Nativity. That commentaries on this text will refer to analogous stories of the births of emperors and kings, replete with heavenly messengers, signs, and widespread hope for peace and prosperity, should be informative to the preacher but not disconcerting. These stories from secular literature are informative in that Luke is a first-century writer, telling his story in a mode familiar enough to be a vehicle for communication. A modern reader is aided in grasping how Luke's first readers understood his Gospel. But these parallel stories should not be disconcerting. Analogies neither prove nor disprove a writer's claim, but they serve to clarify. If a story is such as to be totally without analogy, then who could understand it? Besides, Luke's theology welcomes similar accounts from other cultures. Luke's God is universally available, never without witness among the nations (Acts 14:17). Even pagan poets said, "In him we live and move and have our being" and "For we are indeed his offspring" (Acts 17:28). People everywhere hope and rejoice that the birth of a new leader will bring heaven's blessing of peace and joy.

Luke's witness is that they brought their hopes to Bethlehem and did not go away empty.

The annunciation is to shepherds in the field. We are not sure whether the shepherds are for Luke a continuation of the focus on David who was a shepherd of Bethlehem (I Sam. 16) or a symbol of the poor of the earth who are in Luke the special objects of the grace of God (4:18; 14:13, 21). Both interpretations could be correct. David is a very important figure for Luke, not only in the stories and songs related to the birth of Jesus (1:27, 32, 69; 2:4, 11) but also in the sermons related to the birth of the church (Acts 2:25-35). In Acts, David is presented as a prophet who spoke of Jesus' resurrection and enthronement at God's right hand (II Sam. 7:12-16; Ps. 110:1; 132:11). As to the second interpretation, shepherds were not only poor but of poor reputation, treated religiously and socially almost as non-persons. They qualify easily as the least likely to have God's favor on them, and God's favor on the least likely is a theme throughout the Bible. Israel was the least likely, as was David, and Mary, and Paul, and even Jesus himself. This text certainly provides an opportunity to deal with Jesus' birth through Luke's eyes, quite apart from Matthew who places Jesus' birth among the wise, powerful, and rich. Matthew will speak to the church later, on Epiphany Sunday.

The heavenly host praised God and spoke of peace on earth. Peace (*shalom*), a quality of wholeness in life, made possible by a balance of all the forces within and without which affect us, was always the desire of Israel. The eschatological hope (Isa. 9:6; Zech. 9:9-10) was, says Luke, fulfilled in this one who would "guide our feet into the way of peace" (Luke 1:79). This peace is too immense to be confined to an inner experience, but it is also too personal to be left to the affairs of nations. The preacher will want to give careful attention to the translation of verse 14. Some ancient manuscripts read, "on earth peace, good will among men," a phrase without contingency or condition. The best texts, however, make "good will" a condition for having peace. The phrase may read "among men of good will," "among men with whom he is pleased" (RSV) or "for men on whom his favour rests" (NEB). One must wrestle here not only with texts and translations but with one's own theology.

A brief word about the sign given the shepherds (verse 12). In a field now radiant with heaven, the shepherds are told that the sign is a baby, wrapped as all new born were, and lying in a feed bin for animals. In other words, the sign was as common as the shepherds themselves. Notice Luke's reversal: Earth is not looking to heaven for a sign, but heaven looks to earth. The extraordinary points to the ordinary and says, "See, God is among you."

Christmas, Third Proper (Additional Lessons for Christmas Day)

Isaiah 52:7-10; Psalm 98; Hebrews 1:1-12; John 1:1-14

The readings before us are of two textures, both appropriate for Christmas Day. Both Isaiah 52 and Psalm 98 are expressions of praise to God who comes as king, not only of Israel but also of all the earth. The tone is triumphant. Both Hebrews 1 and John 1, while liturgical and recitative, are theological summaries of the fact and of the meaning of God's son coming into the world. Quite early the church framed its faith so as to be learned, said, and passed on clearly and positively. The tone is reflective.

Isaiah 52:7-10

This lection is especially appropriate for Christmas Day since it concentrates on two features so significant for the season: good tidings and the arrival of a king. A third element, namely the messenger, is also stressed. As is frequently the case with modern ministers, the messenger's importance here derives not from his own person but from the content of his message.

The passage celebrates, in highly exalted fashion, two factors about the God of Israel which can be integrated into the themes of the Christmas Season: God's reign as king and the divine return to Jerusalem.

The text's description of God's reign and return are probably built on the old components of royal processions in which a triumphant monarch returned to the capital city after attaining success in battle. The first component of such an occasion would be the actual victory of the monarch, a feature noted in verse 10. The reference to the bearing of God's holy arm is a way of referring to divine triumph. Note

69

that Deuteronomy 26:8 speaks of God's triumph over the Egyptians in terms of a "mighty hand and an outstretched arm," both symbols of power. Thus the triumphal procession was preceded by a royal victory. The second component was the monarch's return home as the victorious leader. This feature is noted in verse 8 which speaks of Yahweh's return to Zion. The final component of the procession was the acclamation and greeting by the homefolks.

The announcement of good tidings in this text emphasizes the fact that God reigns as king and has triumphed in such a way that the ends of the earth may see the divine salvation. It is interesting to note how the text introduces or speaks about the messenger. It talks about the beauty of the feet of the one who brings good news. Of course, this is an allusion to the common ancient practice of sending messages by runners. The character of the message is what matters most: it concerns peace, tidings of good, the fact of salvation, and the proclamation that God reigns. Just as at Christmastime, it is the angelic good tidings, not the angels themselves, that are of consequence.

The voice of the messenger upon arrival in the city is pictured by the prophet as being joined by the voices of the watchers on the wall who sing together for joy to make known the good news. Finally, even the waste places of Jerusalem, the destroyed parts of the city, are called upon to break forth into singing and celebration.

In spite of this text's affirmation of good news and its great spirit of exaltation, the entire passage has a very poetic quality about it that somewhat removes it from the realm of the mundane and the ordinary. The literalist would want to ask questions about the reality of the changes wrought but such a text as this defies much specificity if read on its own. For Second Isaiah, the triumph of God must be seen as the granting of freedom to the exiles to return home. This is clearly evident in Isaiah 52:11-12, the verses that follow today's Old Testament lection. In these verses, the prophet calls on the people who carry the temple vessels to depart the foreign land and to keep themselves ritually pure, knowing all the time that the God of Israel is their leader as well as their rear guard. The homecoming is thus both for God and for the people.

The Christmas Season can be appreciated and preached as the time when good tidings—even in the face of bad conditions—must be proclaimed. It is also to be preached as a time when God returns to his world, to his own. As in this text, the focus of the season should be on celebration, the joyous response of even the waste places to the assurance that peace, good, salvation and God's rule are the themes of the occasion. Christmas may also be seen as the time when we as people return home—when we return to those true essentials that make a Babe's birth a time of peace and good tidings.

Psalm 98

Like Psalms 96 and 97, this psalm celebrates and proclaims the universal establishment of God's rule and thus represents another expression of the themes found in those psalms as well as in Isaiah 52:7-10. Like Psalm 96, this psalm opens with a call to sing to Yahweh a new song. As a hymn, the psalm is celebrative, oriented to confessional praise, and speaks about, rather than to, the Deity.

The language of the psalm is poetic and while it speaks of divine victory, it does not specify the nature of that victory. Thus, many scholars associate the psalm with the annual celebration of Yahweh's kingship as part of the fall festival.

Verses 1b-3 describe the basis for the excessive celebration called for in the rest of the psalm. As part of God's victory, the divine vindication has been manifest among the nations. That is, the power, might, and reputation of Israel's Deity have been publicly revealed for the nations of the world to behold. This same sentiment can be seen in the star and the Magi of the Christmas story for both reflect the public aspects of God's revelation. God's victory is also the divine way of expressing steadfast love and faithfulness to the house of Israel. Thus God's fidelity to Israel and divine manifestation before the nations are two sides of the same coin.

In the ancient world, a god's reputation was not a foregone conclusion. The welfare of the worshipers of that god and the status of their life and culture were taken as indication of the strength and power of the deity. When people were weak, their god also was considered weak. This is why divine vindication before the nations and divine fidelity to Israel are so closely linked.

Verses 4-6 call on the earth to sing praises to God with various forms of musical instruments. Ancient Israel certainly recognized that there are times when worship and service of the Divine are best expressed in joyful sound and praise and that this is all that is called for. Perhaps the Christmas Season should be viewed as one of those occasions when song and praise are more important than homily and lecture.

In verses 7-8, the poet extends the imaginative imagery and calls on all of nature to function as participants in praise. Four contrasting entities are addressed: the sea with all that lives within it, the whole earth with all those who dwell upon it, the turbulent flood waters that lie deep in the bosom of the earth (see Gen. 7:11; Ps. 93:3), and the hills that reach up toward the heavens. Such extremes are used to emphasize that praise should be rendered by all of the created order—everything in it. (Note that we often use similar language when we speak of people coming from near and far, meaning from "everywhere.")

The celebration before God called for in the psalm is finally based on the assurance that the victorious God comes to judge the earth with righteousness and the peoples with equity. The world is not called on, in other words, to worship and praise a deity who refuses to function as judge or a deity who judges unjustly. The character of God is an important foundation and an essential underpinning of all celebration and praise.

Hebrews 1:1-12

Though the lection ends with verse 12, it should extend through verse 14. The most natural transition occurs after verse 14, as seen by the use of "therefore" in 2:1. The following warning and exhortation (2:1-4) derives directly from the remarks of chapter 1.

This text is truly remarkable in several respects. First, it displays fine literary style, having been deliberately composed to achieve maximum effect as an opening for this impressively argued treatise. The tone of the passage is thoroughly majestic and is meant to be read by an oral interpreter sensitive to style as well as to substance.

Second, it is one of the most definitive statements in the New Testament of Christ's role as the one through whom God has *finally* spoken. As such, it is an important text for the Christian understanding of God's revelation. Set over against the prophetic witnesses through whom God spoke "in many and various ways," Christ is the one through whom God "in these last days" has finally spoken. The multiplicity of their witness is contrasted with the singleness of his. Many voices have now given way to a single voice; the chorus has now given way to the soloist whose appointed time has come to be heard, with the rest, but now above the rest. It should be noted here that the author presupposes that God has never been silent. What has changed is the messenger, who himself is now the message. The major theme of these opening words may be said to be the "God who speaks." If the Old Testament attests the "God who acts," as the biblical theology movement emphasized, so does it present a God who is revealed through words, the words of his prophets then, the word of his Son now.

Third, the passage is remarkable for the truly staggering set of claims it makes about Christ. The Christology here is definitely "high." Several christological images cluster: Christ as the Son of God, and therefore as God's heir; Christ as creator and sustainer of the world; Christ as high priest. In particular, the preexistent work of Christ receives special attention. He is not only the one through whom God created the world (verse 2), but also the one who upholds "the universe by his word of power" (verse 3). Similar emphasis on the creative work of Christ is found in the New Testament (cf. I Cor. 8:6; Col. 1:15-20). Here, however, not only Christ's work, but his nature as well, is defined with respect to God. "He is the radiant light of God's glory and the perfect copy of his nature" (verse 3, JB). Both images are drawn from Alexandrian philosophical traditions. The former image recalls the Genesis creation story and possibly the language of Exodus 24:16; in any case, as God is understood as pure, radiant light, so is Christ understood as essentially light who emanates from God and reflects similar "glory," or brightness. The latter image effectively excludes Christ as, in any sense, a counterfeit copy of God: He is through and through, both in form and substance, an exact replica of God. The reference to his having made "purification for sins," doubtless evokes the image of Christ as high priest, a theme more fully developed later in the treatise (cf. 4:14–7:28).

Fourth, the passage is remarkable for the extended midrash in verses 5-14, where Christ's superiority to angels is elaborated. The chain of seven Old Testament passages (Ps. 2:7; II Sam. 7:14; Deut. 32:43; Ps. 104:4; Ps. 45:6-7; Ps. 102:25-27; Ps. 110:1) are strung together to achieve maximum cumulative effect. Each in its own way shows that by comparison the angels are but "ministering spirits sent forth to serve" humans in obtaining their salvation. Their role is truly subordinate to that of the Son.

This deliberately composed and thoroughly majestic passage, with its singular attention to Christ, is especially well suited as a Christmas text. Even though the role of the preexistent Christ is in the forefront, Advent themes are present. This is especially the case in verse 6: "When he [God] brings the first-born into the world." This appears to be the case in verse 5 as well where Psalm 2:7 is cited. Ordinarily, this psalm is cited in early Christian literature in connection with Christ's resurrection (cf. Acts 13:33; Heb. 5:5; Rom. 1:4). Here, however, it appears that the generation of the Son rather than his resurrection is in view. If this is the correct interpretation, it is indeed surprising.

Clearly, this text reveals an advanced stage of christological reflection, and most likely comes rather late in early Christian thinking about the work of Christ. A wide range of traditions have been drawn upon, most notably wisdom traditions, and in this respect our passage is similar to the Johannine prologue and the Christ hymn in Colossians 1. Obviously, Old Testament texts have exercised a decisive influence on this christological statement, and the catena of Old Testament texts appears to have taken shape at an early stage as the author's predecessors sought to relate the Old Testament witness to Christ. Also noteworthy is verse 8, where Christ is directly addressed as God. Such explicit christological claims by Christians appear not to have been made at the earliest stages. It seems to have taken awhile for such audacity to surface in confessional form.

This text, then, is a richly textured meditation on Christ, striking for the boldness and clarity of its claims. The main stress is on Christ's superiority to the angels, at least as the passage unfolds. Whether the historical situation envisioned here is similar to that addressed in Colossians where Christ's status has been diminished by relegating him to the ranks of all other angelic beings is not clear. Probably not. However, the thrust of the passage is clear: Christ is presented as the preeminent Son of God, without peer within the heavenly hierarchy. This passage is remarkably full of superlatives which reinforce this position of Christ's ultimate supremacy (cf. verses 2-3).

There is a sense in which this staggering set of claims all derive from the one claim of Christ's sonship. If Christ is not *a* son of God but *the* Son of God in an absolute, unqualified sense, the implications are vast. He is indeed "God's heir of all things"; he quite naturally qualifies as God's collaborator in creation and the one who sustains all things by his powerful word.

If Christmas is the one time of the church year when Christians reflect seriously on Christ's sonship and his divine begetting, this text illustrates some of the far-reaching ramifications of such a claim. This point is especially worth making at Christmas, for Christians find it easy to be compelled by seasonal pressure to appropriate the Christ story in only a limited way by celebrating the *birth* of Christ. It is all too easy to romanticize the story of Christ's birth, without realizing the full implications of confessing Christ as *the* Son of God. Our text, however, illustrates the other end of the trajectory, filling out as it does the cosmic implications of belief in the sonship of Christ. Hebrews 1:1-12, therefore, may be said to represent a more mature understanding of Christ to which Christians may advance, even if they have begun with relatively simple meditations on the stories of Christ's birth.

John 1:1-14

The Gospel of John does not have Nativity songs as does Luke, but John does have a hymn to Christ (1:1-18). The Gospel of John does not have a birth story but John does proclaim that the Word became flesh and dwelt among us (1:14). The Gospel of John does not say that the one conceived by the Holy Spirit would be the Son of God, but John does say that the One who became flesh was with God from the beginning, and what God was, he was (1:1). The Gospel of John does not say that God's Son was wrapped in swaddling cloths, lying in a manger, but John does say that the revelation of God in Jesus was concealed if not hidden, veiled in flesh (1:14). John 1:1-14 is, then, an appropriate text for Christmas.

The verses selected for today (1:1-14) are a portion of a unit only slightly larger, 1:1-18, commonly referred to as the prologue. The prologue is clearly a distinct literary unit, having a clear beginning and ending, being poetic in nature in contrast to the prose narrative which follows (1:19ff.), and focusing on a single subject, the Word of God. Because of its unusual literary form and because its presentation of Christ as the Word (Logos) appears nowhere else in the Gospel, some have suggested that 1:1-18 was not an original part of this Gospel. The issue is not a vital one for the preacher because the theological perspective of the prologue is fully congenial with the remainder of the book. In fact, the entire Gospel is in a sense an elaboration upon 1:18: "No one has ever seen God; the only Son, who is in the bosom of the Father, he has made him known."

John 1:1-18 consists of three stanzas with two insertions about John the Baptist (verses 6-8, 15). (For comments on these verses, see Third Sunday of Advent.) The first stanza, verses 1-5, relates God to all creation through the Word, the second, verses 9-13, relates God to human life through the Word, and the third, verses 14-18, provides the divine offer of grace and truth through the Word. It is not abortive of meaning to conclude at verse 14 as does this lection, since verse 14 is John's "Christmas story" in capsule, but because verses 14-18 are the affirmation of faith (among us, we have beheld, we have all received) concluding the hymn, the sermon properly should embrace the whole of the Prologue.

A preacher may recoil at the thought of a single sermon on the entire text, and properly so. Its scope is immense: all creation, Israel, the Baptist movement, the church, pre-existence of the Word, and salvation through the revelation of the Word. In addition, the passage is not only hymnic but polemic, contending with the synagogue and the followers of the Baptist (verses 6-8, 15, 17). But for the occasion of Christmas, one would do well to step back and see the whole of it. Sometimes enabling listeners to sense the size and grandeur of a text is of more value than detailed application to their lives.

Let us, then, allow the Fourth Evangelist to tell us the Good News. A fundamental human hunger is to know God. "Show us the Father, and we shall be satisfied" (14:8). In fact, to know God is life eternal (17:3). But no one has ever seen God (1:18), and even though God is the creator and sustainer of all life and available to obedient faith (1:1-12), knowledge of God does not come by observation or by the accumulation of proofs. However, since God is gracious toward the world (3:16), the darkness of ignorance and death are dispelled by the coming of the Son as revealer (1:18). In order to tell this story, John borrows a category familiar to Jewish and Greek culture, Word or Logos (the feminine synonym often interchanged with Logos is Sophia, Wisdom). The Word or Wisdom through which God created and sustains the world (Gen. 1:3; Ps. 33:4-7; Heb. 1:3) came to be personified in late Judaism as a separate being (Prov. 8; Wisd. 7; Sir. 24). In Sirach, for example, this Wisdom through whom God created the world asked of God permission to come dwell on earth. Permission was granted, but the earth was evil, foolish, and inhospitable. And so God made Wisdom to become a book, the Book of Moses, to dwell in the tents of Jacob (Sir. 24). But for the Evangelist, the eternal Wisdom or Word becomes not a book but flesh, a person, Jesus of Nazareth.

Not all who met Jesus experienced God, nor do they today, but to all who do, God gives "power to become children of God" (1:12).

First Sunday After Christmas

Isaiah 61:10–62:3; Psalm 111; Galatians 4:4-7;
Luke 2:22-40

In Jesus Christ God has done a new thing, but our texts for this Sunday offer us two important reminders: First, what God has done in Jesus is a fulfillment of and not a departure from God's work in the past. Luke portrays a young Jesus being reared according to the law of Moses, and Paul concurs in Galatians 4: Jesus was born of woman, under the law. Second, God's act of redemption is still in process (Isa.) and calls for a response of obedience and thanksgiving (Ps.). This Sunday is after Christmas but it is also before Epiphany.

Isaiah 61:10–62:3

Portions of this lection were also part of the Old Testament reading for the Third Sunday of Advent. The fact that the passage stresses salvation as already partially realized as well as anticipated make it appropriate for an Advent reading. As a post-Christmas reading, its emphasis on the experience of salvation, its interest in the nations, and its focus on Zion make it appropriate as a text that looks forward to Epiphany.

The lection clearly breaks down in two distinct units. The first in 61:10-11 is a joyful response celebrating the salvation which God has brought about or at least promised. Perhaps the "I" of verse 10 is the prophet speaking or probably more likely it is a personified embodiment of the community. Two images are drawn upon to give expression to the experience and anticipation of salvation. The first, in verse 10, utilizes aspects associated with the joy of a wedding ceremony— salvation is a garment in which the saved are decked out like the bride and bridegroom adorned in the finery and wealth of their wedding garments. Israel as the bride of God is of course a common emphasis in many of the books of the prophets (Hos. 1–3; Jer. 2:1-3). Many of the sayings and parables of Jesus likewise draw upon wedding imagery. The minister might think about this text in terms of a sermon on salvation as a wedding. The second image, in verse 11, draws upon agricultural phenomena. The assurance that God will make righteousness and praise spring forth before the nations is compared to how the land or a garden causes to grow what has been planted in it. The salvation and the assurance may be no more than seeds lying in the soil but as the farmer has the certainty of growth and harvest so the Word of God brings with it the certainty of salvation. Again, the imagery of sowing and harvesting is significant in many of Jesus' sayings and parables.

The second portion of the lection, Isaiah 62:1-3, really goes with what follows in the remainder of chapter 62 more than with the preceding chapter. The reference to the nations and the kings seeing the glory of Zion gives this text a connection with the approaching Epiphany Season.

In 62:1-3, we encounter the prophet as intercessor before God on behalf of the people. Although the character of the prophetic office tended to stress the prophet as one who spoke for God and addressed Israel, the prophet also spoke for Israel and addressed God. In this second function, the prophet was the people's representative before, and intercessor with, God (see Amos 7:1-6; Jer. 7:16; Ezek. 13:1-5).

The prophet declares in 62:1 that he will not be kept silent but will pester and intercede with the Deity until Jerusalem has experienced a salvation that can be seen as clearly as a bright light or a burning torch. Obviously the prophet seems set on overcoming some skepticism in the community about whether the coming salvation is certain or not. The prophetic promise of incessant intercession thus functions as a word of assurance to the community. The minister could focus a sermon on the importance and role of intercession and intercessory prayer, stressing the fact that intercession gives expression to the common bonds that bind all humanity together and provides a means of touching the Deity on behalf of others. Being intercessors on behalf of others also provides the ones interceding with a new perspective on themselves.

In addressing Zion, in verses 2-3, the prophet assures the city that nations will eventually see her vindication and kings her glory. (This theme of course can be viewed as analogous to the coming of the Wise Men at the birth of Jesus.) Jerusalem will be given a new name by God as the sign of the city's transformation from a desolate, dissipated place (see Isa. 62:4-5, 12) to become a crown of beauty and a royal diadem. The fact that God is to give the name carries with it extra significance for it indicates that the new status and the new circumstances are divinely ordained.

Psalm 111

This psalm is a thanksgiving psalm although its content is primarily a hymn of praise. In ancient Israelite worship, the individual or community offered thanksgiving after some calamity had passed or after a rescue from some state of distress. As a rule, thanksgiving psalms generally contain more material that is addressed to a human audience than is addressed directly to the Deity. Thanksgiving psalms were, therefore, a way of offering one's testimony. This, of course, is the exact opposite of the lament psalms which fundamentally contain only address to the Deity. Thanksgiving psalms were thus primarily intended for the worshiping audience more than for the Deity. Psalm 111, although setting out to give thanks to the Lord, contains no direct address to God.

That this psalm was used in a context of thanksgiving is clear from the opening verse as is the fact that the thanksgiving was offered in public worship—"in the company of the upright, in the congregation." The psalm, unlike most thanksgivings, contains no reference to the distress from which the one offering thanks may have been saved or to any special reason for offering thanks.

In fact, what we have in the psalm, following the opening verse, is a hymn of praise extolling the works of God and the divine fidelity to the covenant. That a thanksgiving takes the form of a hymn should not surprise us.

The psalm in the lectionary is a good balance to the other

Old Testament lection providing thanksgiving and praise as the response to the proclamation of salvation in Isaiah 61:10–62:3.

The works of God singled out in the psalm for praise are declared both worthy of study and of remembrance (verses 2-4). The works or acts of God are seen as the deeds of Israel's sacred history. Three special acts are recalled. There is, first of all, the giving of food for those who fear the Divine (verse 5). This verse seems to allude, although not with absolute certainty, to the protection and care for Israel in the wilderness when the people were fed with quails and manna (see Exod. 16:13-35). Second, God displayed great power in giving the Israelites the land of Canaan as "the heritage of the nations" (verse 6). Finally, there is reference throughout the psalm to the covenant that was given at Sinai (see verses 5, 7-9). The twofold stress of verse 9 emphasizes both the redemption of God and the commands of the covenant. Or we could say that the psalmist is declaring that in the redemptive acts of the past and in the commands of the covenant, one possesses the means to study and remember in obedience the works and ways of God (verses 2, 4). Such study should lead to the fear of God which is the beginning of wisdom (verse 10).

In the Christian tradition, the incarnation, celebrated in the birth of Jesus, is a mighty work of God but it is also a work which demands our study and remembrance as well as obedient responsiveness. Acts of salvation must be responded to, and just as those acts on behalf of ancient Israel were viewed as obligating Israel to faithful obedience so the act of God in Christ obligates the Christian to a life of fidelity.

Galatians 4:4-7

This text from Galatians, with its dual emphasis on Christ as God's Son and, by extension, Christians as God's sons, or children, effectively extends themes celebrated at Christmas. Paul's statement that Christ was "born of woman" (verse 4), in one sense, serves as a hinge connecting this reading with the Lukan birth narratives read earlier for the Fourth Sunday of Advent and for Christmas Eve/Christmas Day. It also fits well with today's Gospel text which is the final section of the Lukan birth narrative.

It is worth noting that this is one of Paul's rare references to an event in the life of the historical Jesus. To be sure, the language is traditional, yet it shows that Paul was not totally uninterested in this first stage of Christ's earthly ministry. Some scholars have seen here a cryptic reference to the tradition of Jesus' virgin birth ("born of woman—not man," as both Matthew and Luke attest), which is otherwise not mentioned in the Pauline Letters. However formulaic the language here, it fully conforms to Paul's insistence elsewhere on Christ's full humanity (cf. Phil. 2:5-11).

Since most of the earlier epistolary readings to this point have been drawn from the non-Pauline and deutero-Pauline Letters, this might be an appropriate occasion to explore this aspect of Paul's Christology. Some of the Pauline passages treating the humanity of Christ include Romans 1:3; 7:4; 9:5; I Corinthians 15:21; II Corinthians 8:9; Philippians 2:7-8; also cf. Colossians 2:9.

In similar fashion, the phrase "born under the law" might be explored in direct connection with the Gospel lesson for today (Luke 2:22-40), where Jesus' parents are portrayed as faithful adherents to the Mosaic law (cf. Luke 2:39). The final section of the Lukan birth narrative (Luke 2:41-52) also presents Jesus as a young man being nurtured in the traditions of his parents. Naturally, Jesus' Jewishness raises critical issues concerning the relation between law and gospel. Paul's arguments in Galatia have influenced Christian thought to draw a sharp distinction between "bondage under the law" and "freedom in the gospel." Here, however, Christ's solidarity with his Jewish past is asserted, and this might be used to explore the lines of continuity between Christianity and Judasm.

In verses 5b-7, the newly obtained status of sonship is obviously the central point. The opening phrase, "because you are sons" (verse 6), is emphatic and unequivocal. As confirming testimony to the reality of this new status, "God has sent the Spirit of his Son into our hearts, crying, 'Abba! Father!' " "Spirit" here is doubtless the Holy Spirit, and its close association with Christ is not unusual for Paul (cf. Rom. 8).

Paul conceives of Christ's Spirit as the catalyst within every Christian working to bring about the filial obedience that typified the work of Christ himself. "Abba! Father!" is one of the few instances outside the gospel tradition where the literal words of Jesus are preserved in their original Aramaic form. This in itself signifies the importance of these words uttered by the historical Jesus. So memorably did they symbolize Christ's willingness to fulfill his commitment to be Son of God in an absolute sense that the early church preserved them as originally spoken. With these words we are not only hearing Jesus' own language of prayer, but as the text suggests, the prayers of the early Christians as they besought the Spirit of Christ to bring about in them the quality of pristine obedience they understood the death of Christ to represent. The interior quality of Christ's life of sonship is now envisioned as a reality for every one of God's "sons." No longer is such a level of sonship something for which we must wait, it is the legacy of every one who is in Christ. The Christian's task is not to wait any longer for this legacy, but to lay claim to it now, in the "fulness of time," when God's eschatological work has already begun.

This text, then, read the First Sunday After Christmas, might be developed profitably in several directions. First, one might wish to focus on Paul's particular way of dealing with Christ's humanity, contrasting this with the more extended narrative treatments of the Gospels. Second, one might wish to focus on Christians' status as God's children, adopted yet nonetheless full heirs. It might be noted here that in dealing with this passage, it will be more difficult to use inclusive language. "God's child/children" will usually do double duty for "God's Son/sons," but it is easy to lose the subtlety of the Pauline play on words—Christ as God's Son, Christians as God's sons—especially taking seriously the adoption metaphor. Third, the unusual occurrence of "Abba!" with all the attention it has received in recent years, offers many possibilities (cf. Rom. 8:15). One might easily develop the theme of the profile of "sonship" that results as one gradually learns to make Jesus' prayer, "Abba! Father!"

one's own. Or, the role of the Spirit as the enabling agent in bringing about this life of obedience is equally suitable and homiletically productive. In either case, the liberating power of Christ's work remains a central theme.

Luke 2:22-40

Whether the Sunday after Christmas is a significant time or merely the occasion for picking up the twelve baskets of fragments depends very much on the minister. If the minister understands that the congregation does not always have to be at high tide but may experience ebb and flow in good health, then this Sunday can be anticipated as an important time for preaching. In fact, just as many welcome meat and potatoes after surfeiting on holiday goodies, so might a solid offering from the pulpit be warmly received. We are indebted to Luke for a text that speaks to us after shepherds, angels, and heavenly hosts are gone. Mary and Joseph have a son to rear, religious obligations to keep, and a trip back to Nazareth to make. Sounds familiar enough.

The Gospel lesson for today, Luke 2:22-40, serves at least four purposes for the author. First, even in his infancy Jesus' life was characterized as being in full obedience to the law of Moses. Even in this brief text, that fact is stated no less than five times (verses 22, 23, 24, 27, 39). The particular forms of that obedience consisted of circumcision, which Luke combined with the naming according to the angel's instruction (verses 21; 1:31); the dedication of the firstborn to God (Exod. 13:1-2); and the purification of the mother (Lev. 12:6). Because of the family's poverty, they were allowed to sacrifice according to the law's special provision (Lev. 12:8). For the purposes of his narration Luke has related the dedication and purification as one event. (For an earlier story of a mother giving her son to God, see I Sam. 1–2.) By stating repeatedly that the law was being observed, Luke was saying that Jesus was a true Israelite. Circumcision, dedication, purification of the mother, to the temple at age twelve, public life at age thirty, in the synagogue on the sabbath as was his custom: these and other proofs of Jesus' commitment to the law are given by Luke. And in Acts, the church continued synagogue and temple attendance, and Paul went first to the synagogue in every city and went through vow ceremonies in Jerusalem at the request of church leaders there. In other words, says Luke, Jesus and the church are no renegade splinter movement, flaunting freedom as disobedience to the law. Rather, in Jesus and the church Judaism is properly continued and fulfilled. Jesus worked within and through his tradition; he threw no stones from a distance.

A second purpose fulfilled by Luke in 2:22-40 is the declaration of the Child's greatness. At birth the declaration was by an angel, at age twelve by the teachers of the law (2:46-47), and at the beginning of his ministry by the voice from heaven (3:22). Here it is by two aged, pious Jews, Simeon and Anna. Simeon was inspired by the Holy Spirit (verses 25-27) to recognize in the infant Jesus the fulfillment of his hope. His waiting was for the consolation of Israel (Isa. 40:1) but he foresaw that Jesus would be a center of controversy, the occasion for the fall and rise of many in Israel (an allusion to the stone that would aid or cause to stumble, Isa. 28:16) and a cause of piercing grief to his mother (verses 34-35). Anna, a prophetess, was a widow (the Greek is unclear whether she was eighty-four or had been a widow eighty-four years), and as such belonged to a class well known in Israel (Naomi, Judith) and in the early church where their duties included prayer night and day (I Tim. 5:3-10). Through these two Luke may be saying that Israel, when led by the Spirit, righteous, and devoted to prayer and fasting, could see in Jesus the fulfillment of her longing.

A third purpose of this passage is to return the family and the action of the narrative to Galilee and to Nazareth. Luke will later present Jesus announcing the nature and purpose of his ministry in a synagogue in Nazareth, "where he had been brought up" (4:16). For now, and for the next twelve years, it is enough to say "the child grew and became strong, filled with wisdom; and the favor of God was upon him" (2:40).

A fourth and final purpose of this text is to introduce another Christian hymn, the "Nunc Dimittis" (verses 29-32). Like the other hymns Luke has used in chapters 1–2, this one consists of phrases and lines from the Hebrew Scriptures, mostly Isaiah 49 and 52. The song speaks of the fading of the old before the new, the realization of hope, and God's final embrace of all peoples, Jew and Gentile.

If the preacher needs an image for this last Sunday of the year, here it is: an old man holding a baby.

January 1 (When Observed as New Year's Eve or Day)

Ecclesiastes 3:1-13; Psalm 8; Colossians 2:1-7; Matthew 9:14-17

These texts address beautifully but firmly those persons poised on January 1 between the old and the new. The writer of Ecclesiastes is so caught on the cycle of the seasons and the ceaseless turn of time that the only word is to try to live in harmony with time's flow. If passing time brings a sense of futility and diminished worth, the psalmist has an uplifting word about humanity's likeness to God. Matthew reminds his readers that there is such a thing as a radically new life, quite different from the old, and Paul urges his Colossian readers to live that new life in words, deeds, and relationships.

Ecclesiastes 3:1-13

It is appropriate that one of the lections for the new year be this passage from Ecclesiastes, although in many ways this is a very pessimistic text. But then, of course, so is practically the whole Book of Ecclesiastes.

This text is concerned with time and the proper occasions for doing things and also with the continuously repeated round and routine of human experience and existence. Like the content of this passage, the passing of every old year and the beginning of every new year ought to make us more time-conscious as well as more aware that both time and events have their occasion and their season and that to act at the proper time is a matter of great insightfulness and is not the consequence of merely moving through life without thought.

The opening verse of this chapter lays out an abstract thesis: everything has its season and there is a proper time for every matter under the heavens. The wisdom poem that follows in verses 2-8 illustrates the abstract reality by a series of concrete examples. Fourteen pairs of antithetical actions are stated in order to illustrate the general principle. The poem presents life and the routines of existence as occasions for action, though the proper type of action required is neither random nor open. Thus this text views human life as predetermined in many ways. That is, if one is to act successfully, then the timing of the act must meet the real opportunity and need of the occasion. Human action, according to this text, is not a matter of absolute freedom. The success of an action must recognize the limitations placed on the action and the necessity to fit the action to the needs and opportunities of the occasion.

The Old Testament, especially in the wisdom books, stresses the need for word and action to be appropriate to the occasion—the proper action on the proper occasion. Note the following texts:

> To make an apt answer is a joy to a man,
>   and a word in season, how good it is! (Prov. 15:23)

> A word fitly spoken
>   is like apples of gold in a setting of silver. (Prov. 25:11)

Isaiah 28:23-29 emphasizes that in agricultural pursuits one has to perform the right tasks at the proper time. A new year's sermon could build on the theme of the proper time by emphasizing the necessity to correlate actions and occasions so that the two blend together harmoniously. For one to correlate action and occasion to produce that which is most appropriate requires close attention to all the circumstances and a weighing of the consequences of actions on the circumstances. Otherwise one may end up weeping when laughter is called for or dancing when one should be mourning.

The old poem in verses 1-8 appears to have been taken over by the author of Ecclesiastes who then dialogues with its content by presenting an even more pessimistic reading of the human opportunites which the occasions in life present. Verses 9-13 suggest that God has predetermined everything to such an extent that humans are really rather powerless before the determinations of God. Verse 9 suggests that if things are going to happen in a divinely determined way there is nothing that the doer of an action can do to add anything that makes a difference. God has assigned humans their tasks, "made everything beautiful in its time" (or better, "made each thing right for its time"), but humans do not have the capacity to find out what God has done or will be doing. Verse 11 in the RSV states that God "has put eternity" into human minds thus rendering them incapable of understanding God. The word translated eternity might also be rendered "enigma," "obscurity," "the unknown." In spite of how one translates the word, the sense is clear: Humans may have inquiring minds but they do not possess the capacity to understand the activity of God.

In light of this rather pessimistic reading of time and human understanding, the author of Ecclesiastes offers an evaluation or approach to the situation: The best thing people can do in life is to be happy and enjoy themselves and take pleasure in whatever occupation or toil comes their way. Although such a philosophy produces a rather diminished vision of human achievement, it nonetheless stresses an important factor about life: Happiness and pleasure should be sought and enjoyed amid the toils and occupations of life (see Eccles. 2:24-25; 3:22; 9:7-10; 11:8). Happiness and pleasure are also gifts of God and should be enjoyed wherever they may be found in the normal course of living.

Psalm 8

The contents and emphasis of this lection are almost completely the opposite of Ecclesiastes 3:1-13. The latter presents humanity almost at the mercy of divine determinism. Psalm 8, however, stresses the exalted position of humanity in God's created order, although it too can speak of the human sense of insignificance when confronted with the created universe. Both these emphases, the greatness and glory of humanity and yet its sense of insignificance when viewed in light of the divine might and majesty, can be combined in a sermon and the minister can have the two lections dialogue with each other, recognizing the truth in both positions.

While it is true that Psalm 8 sees humanity in a more exalted status than practically any other biblical text, nonetheless, the focus of the psalm is praise of a God who created the world and conferred on humanity a position of honor and responsibility exceeding that of any other created being. (Note that Eccles. 3:19 declares that humans have no real advantage over animals in that both end up with the same fate.) This praise of God as the purpose of the psalm can be seen in its (1) hymnic quality, (2) in the fact that it is a hymn directly addressed to the Deity which is a very rare feature of biblical hymns (for another example, see Ps. 104), and (3) in the use of identical praises in the prelude and the postlude. Thus what the psalm has to say about both the insignificance and the status of humanity is a way of praising the Deity.

Verses 1*b*-2 present innumerable problems both to the translator and the exegete although the sense of the text seems to be that babes and infants recognize and testify to the greatness of God (see Matt. 21:16) and that their testimony puts at rest any enemy or avenger. Babes see the truth that other miss.

Verses 3-4 give expression to that universal feeling of humanity's inconsequential status when confronted with the broad sweep of the night skies dotted with the moon and the stars. (One should note that in antiquity, when pollution was so much less and artificial lighting was nil, the skies at night must have been even more splendid and awesome than they appear today.) Confronted with the lighted canopy of the heavens, humans almost naturally sense their littleness and wonder why God could be concerned for something so small. If the ancients felt this way, how much more we moderns who have seen the earth from outer space and are aware of the vastness of the regions beyond our solar system. (With a universe so large does it ultimately matter if we ordered English peas and instead were served green beans?)

Over against the sense of human insignificance, Psalm 8 affirms the high status of human existence. Humans are created only a little lower than God who has placed the whole of creation under human dominion. The works of God's hands are placed beneath the feet of humankind. Humanity thus serves as God's vice-regent over the whole of creation.

In preaching from Psalm 8, and especially when combined with Ecclesiastes 3:1-13, the preacher should focus on the paradoxical nature and situation of humans in the world. Opposite poles—human lowliness and human heights—are held in tension because both reflect realities of the true situation. Humankind, this mortal creature of insignificance, overshadowed by the vastness of the sky's canopy, is also the one possessing dominion over the whole of the divine creation and sharing in the divine dignity.

Colossians 2:1-7

This passage belongs closely with the preceding verses (1:24-29), where Paul has elaborated his own apostolic understanding in general terms. With 2:1, he turns his attention more directly to the Colossians' own situation. This passage is also a prelude to the frontal assault of the heresy confronting the Colossians (2:8-23). Several allusions foreshadow his treatment of the heretical teaching.

He hopes that his readers will "have all the riches of assured understanding and the knowledge of God's mystery of Christ" (verse 2). This reassurance is calculated to offset the effects of gnostic teaching through which such esoteric knowledge becomes the property of only an elite minority. His insistence that Christ is the one "in whom are hid all the treasures of wisdom and knowledge" (verse 3) has similar force, and recalls the magnificent Christ-hymn of Colossians 1:15-20. It serves to counter the charges of those who regard Christ as yet another heavenly power in the angelic hierarchy. His readers are warned against deceitful teachers who use "beguiling speech" (verse 4). This darker side of rhetorical ability Paul had already addressed in I Corinthians 2, and his conviction that sophistic speech profits little is restated in Colossians 2:8.

These sober instructions are given from a distance. Many of his readers are unknown to him personally (2:1), yet his concern for them is not diminished by distance. Indeed, his "spirit" is with them (verse 5), and news that their faith in

Christ is in "good order" and "firm" is an occasion for him to rejoice (verse 5). The overall tone of the passage should be noticed, however, for it reflects the sober realism of an apostle who understands that faith is never static but constantly vulnerable to outside erosion. But the response is not cold and reactionary. It is rather crafted recognizing that matters of faith and fidelity are deeply personal and can only be successfully adjudicated through effective moral and personal suasion.

These words in the opening section, written at a distance yet full of genuine concern, set up his final set of remarks in verses 6-7, at the heart of which is the emphatic imperative: "live in him" (verse 6). In fact, these two verses vividly illustrate the "indicative-imperative" pattern so typical of early Christian parenesis. The indicative is succinctly, yet powerfully stated: "As therefore you received Christ Jesus the Lord." Out of this directly follows the imperative: "so live in him."

"Receive" here is to be understood in a fully existential sense. As Romans 10:9 indicates, such "reception" involves both confession with the mouth and believing with the heart, hence an act involving the whole person. "Christ Jesus as Lord" embodies the early Christian confession, yet has even greater impact here in light of the preeminent lordship attributed to Christ in the magnificent Christ-hymn in Colossians 1:15-20. The injunction to live "in him" defines the sphere in which the Christian imperative is to be carried out, but more than this it states the motive and agent for Christian ethics. Pauline exhortation is frequently defined as "in the Lord" (cf. Eph. 6:1; Col. 3:18), and it is clear that "the Lord" is not only *where* Christian behavior is anchored, but *how* it is achieved. This emphasis is further developed in the three participles that follow: "rooted . . . built up . . . established." Agricultural and architectural metaphors are combined here (cf. I Cor. 3:9). The clear implication is that the all-encompassing fullness of Christ is sufficiently deep as the soil in which Christians can sink deep roots; or, to shift the metaphor, sufficiently sturdy as a foundation on which they can build. "Established in the faith" refers to instructional matters, and faith is used here in the sense of "the teaching of the church" rather than in the existential sense in which Paul uses the term in Romans. "Just as you were taught" stresses the continuity between their earlier reception and growth in faith and the task before them of confronting competing faith-systems. The final participle "abounding in thanks-giving" enjoins the readers to adopt a stance toward life typified in the opening prayer (Col. 1:3-8).

One can scarcely imagine a more suitable text, especially verses 6-7, for a Christian meditation or sermon at the new year. The first section, with its emphasis on the richness and fullness of the mystery of Christ, the all-encompassing character of "the treasures of wisdom and knowledge" can be used in virtually the same way by modern Christian preachers and teachers as Paul used it then—to remind Christians that the Christ whom they have "received as Lord" and in whom they live is an unfathomable resource for spiritual knowledge and strength. The second section (verses 6-7) is so universally apt that the preacher can make the hermeneutical leap virtually without modification. It is one of those instances where the New Testament has caught so successfully the essence of universal Christian faith that its best form of appropriation is mere restatement. Accordingly, it can be spoken by the Christian minister to the congregation as effectively and as directly now as it was then. In fact, a sermon could easily be developed in midrashic fashion through which the main phrases become the major divisions of the sermon itself.

Matthew 9:14-17

Reflection upon the old and the new and upon issues related to change is unavoidable as December 31 becomes January 1. The calendar functions to bring to our attention in a sobering way how profoundly complex are questions that cluster around the relation of old and new, questions that are historical, theological, and personal. Matthew, too, wrestled with these issues as our Gospel lection for today makes clear.

Matthew 9:14-17 is a part of the larger unit, 9:1-17, in which Matthew follows closely the first three of Mark's five conflict stories (2:1–3:6): forgiving sin, eating with sinners, and fasting. Apparently Matthew places the question about fasting (verses 14-17) in the same setting as the question about eating with sinners, a dinner at which Jesus sat with publicans and sinners (9:10). At that meal, Pharisees asked Jesus' disciples why he ate with sinners, and Jesus responded. The question about fasting was posed by disciples of John (in Mark, "people" asked him) and was directed to Jesus concerning his disciples. Again Jesus responded. It is appropriate that disciples of John ask about fasting since their leader was an ascetic, neither eating nor drinking (Matt. 11:18). Eating habits were of social and religious importance and created problems for both John ("He has a demon") and Jesus ("Behold, a glutton and a drunkard," 11:18-19). The question involves three religious communities which are seeking to do God's will: the synagogue, the Baptist movement, and the church.

The passage consists of the question and Jesus' answer. The heart of the answer is Jesus' pronouncement framed as a rhetorical question: "Can the wedding guests mourn [Mark has "fast"] as long as the bridegroom is with them?" The clear implication is that the presence of Jesus is the presence of the kingdom. The image of bridegroom and wedding feast, familiar to Judaism and early Christianity, conveys the spirit of joy and celebration appropriate to the kingdom. Most scholars regard the second half of Jesus' answer, "The days will come . . . and then they will fast" (verse 15b), as the church's understanding of Jesus' position on fasting. In other words, in looking to Jesus for a defense of its own life and practices, the church recognized a difference between its situation and that of Jesus but found in Jesus a justification for that difference. Jesus and his disciples did not fast, witnessing rather to the joy appropriate to the presence of the kingdom in the person of Jesus. Later the church did practice fasting (Matt. 6:16-18; Acts 13:2-3) but that, too, was appropriate since the bridegroom had been taken from them. Jesus thus defends in verse 15 both his immediate and his future followers. Fasting as a Christian practice will receive more attention in the Gospel lesson for Ash Wednesday.

The remainder of today's lesson consists of two originally independent proverbs or maxims about garments and wineskins (verses 16-17). They fit into the context in that they serve as a general defense of Christian innovations in worship and community life. Simply to attach Christianity to Judaism (patch) or to try to continue life after Jesus as it had been before (old wineskins) would be destructive both to Judaism and Christianity.

One can sense here as elsewhere in Matthew the difficulties in negotiating old and new. Both personally and historically, Jesus is a new beginning, that is, fixed in the biblical witness and in human experience. But this does not have to be proven by never visiting the quarry from which we were mined, by denying tradition, by refusing to recognize Abraham and Sarah as our parents. Every New Testament writer struggled with the continuity and discontinuity between the church and the synagogue. In Matthew's church one issue was fasting. No, says Matthew, Jesus and his group did not fast but not in stubborn revolt; they witnessed to the joy of the messianic banquet. Yes, says Matthew, our church practices fasting, but not in imitation of Judaism in many quarters of which it had become empty display. We fast as an appropriate response to the death of the Messiah and to our struggle to be faithful in awaiting his return.

Every minister knows how painful change can be. Even a minor alteration in the order of worship is for some very disorienting. Perhaps changes remind us too vividly of our mortality, but changes do and should come, and the minister often has to initiate them. But never with laughter.

Second Sunday After Christmas

Jeremiah 31:7-14 or Ecclesiasticus 24:1-4, 12-16; Psalm 147:12-20;
Ephesians 1:3-6, 15-18; John 1:1-18

The preacher will notice that Jeremiah 31 and Psalm 147 are similar in their praise of God's faithfulness in dealing with the weary and scattered people of faith. Ecclesiasticus 24, Ephesians 1, and John 1 are likewise similar in that all three declare that God's work of redemption and revelation began before creation. In Ecclesiasticus God revealed, created, and redeemed through Sophia or Wisdom, and in John, through Logos, or the Word. Ephesians agrees, insisting that both Christ and God's plan for our salvation are eternal, not contingent upon the world's favor or opposition.

Jeremiah 31:7-14

In 722 B.C., Shalmaneser the Assyrian King, (727–722 B.C.) and his forces captured Samaria the Israelite capital city. The town had defended itself against the Assyrian siege for three years even though the Israelite king Hoshea had been imprisoned by the Assyrians before the siege began (see II Kings 17:1-6). Obviously the Israelite population had strongly supported the rebellion from Assyria and saw in their efforts an opportunity to secure national independence.

Shalmaneser died shortly after Samaria was taken. Apparently with his death, the main Assyrian army returned home where Sargon (722–705 B.C.) became the new monarch.

In spite of their recent defeat, the Israelites resumed their rebellion and rose up in defiance against the new Assyrian monarch. In an Assyrian cuneiform text uncovered in excavations in the early 1950s, Sargon reports the following about his handling of the old Northern Kingdom of Israel and its capital at Samaria:

27,280 people with their chariots and the gods they trust, as spoil I counted, 200 chariots of theirs I included in my army . . . . The city of Samaria I restored, and greater than before I rebuilt it. Peoples of other lands I settled within it; my official as ruler I placed over them; and together with the people of Assyria I counted them.

In this text, Sargon tells of capturing the city and taking away its gods (probably the items associated with religion such as the calf built by Jeroboam; see Hos. 10:5-6). The city was rebuilt, partially resettled with foreigners, and the region became a part of the Assyrian empire with a military governor.

Sargon claims to have carried over 27,000 Israelites into exile. We don't know if this number included only the males or everyone. If it were only male heads of households then the number would be three or four times larger. From the beginning of the reign of Tiglath-pileser III (745–727) to the end of the reign of Ashurbanipal (668–627), over three and a half million persons were deported and exiled by the Assyrians.

Most of us in the Western world of today do not realize the trauma either of being exiled or of watching family/friends being deported and settled elsewhere. Many aging parents in the ancient world watched their children led away and spent the rest of their lives hoping to see them again. Every caravan that arrived from afar was greeted with the hope that loved ones were returning home.

In Jeremiah 30–31, we possess what has been called the prophet's Book of Comfort, two chapters concerned with the return of exiles to their homeland. Jeremiah 31:1-22 speaks of the return from exile of northern Israelites and their renewed life in the land. Even though Jeremiah preached over a hundred years after the exile of northerners, the hope of their return still remained alive.

In verses 7-14, Jeremiah speaks of the assurance that exiles will return and of the nature of their renewed life in the land. Several matters are noteworthy in this text.

1. *Celebration as response.* Jeremiah's audience is called on to celebrate, in advance, the return and restoration of exiles. (Part of the celebration associated with Christmas is

celebration in advance, celebration of Easter already at Christmas.) Note the number of verbs emphasizing rejoicing and celebrating in verse 7:

> Cry out in joy for Jacob,
> Shout at the crossroads of the nations!
> Sing aloud in praise, and say:
> Save, O Lord, Your people,
> The remnant of Israel. (NJPSV)

(The RSV reading, "The Lord has saved his people," is based on changing an imperative verb to a normal perfect or past tense.)

2. *The nature of redemption.* In verses 8-9, the extent of the return is noted. Exiles will come from the ends of the earth: the north country and the farthest parts of the world. There will be a great company even including those whom one would normally not expect on a journey: the lame, the blind, the pregnant, and the newborn (instead of the RSV's "her who is in travail"). The return will be characterized by weeping (for joy), consolation (or compassion), and a journey eased by refreshing brooks for rest stops and a level road (or straight path) for safe travel.

3. *Proclamation among the nations.* Ephraim's deliverance and return will be proclaimed among the nations of the world. For the Northern Kingdom, Jeremiah uses the old tribal name Ephraim, the region in which the capital was located. Firstborn denotes here "favorite" (see Exod. 4:22). Just as the firstborn who had to be ransomed (see Exod. 13:11-13), so Ephraim would be ransomed and reclaimed from the strong hands of the oppressor who had exiled him. What Jeremiah here proclaims is that Ephraim would be restored to its old status.

4. *The nature of the restored life.* In verses 12-14, Jeremiah describes the conditions that will prevail in the days of salvation to come. (a) Zion/Jerusalem will be the place where even the northerners worship, as in the days of David and Solomon. (b) People will be radiant over the blessings of Yahweh—the grain, wine, oil, and newborn of the flock. The minister, in preaching on this text, should note that the ideal future is not some out-of-this-world, miraculous existence

but the return to normalcy. The blessings, however, are received with joy and thanksgiving. (c) Life will be like a watered garden, always productive and bearing. (d) Rejoicing would be characteristic of life. "Then shall maidens dance gaily, / Young men and old alike" (NJPSV). Dancing is taken in the Bible as one of the surest expressions of joy and well-being. (Like exercise, dancing is the natural enemy of depression.) (e) The section closes with Yahweh's promise to reverse the patterns of past existence—mourning to joy, gladness to sorrow. Even the clergy would enjoy "their fill of fatness" (NJPSV) since the priests would share in the people's sacrifices that would follow on their receipt of bounty.

Ecclesiasticus 24:1-4, 12-16

The book of Ecclesiasticus (or the Wisdom of Jesus the Son of Sirach) was part of the Bible of the Medieval Church but was dropped from the canon by Luther and the other reformers. Originally written in Hebrew about 190 B.C., the work was translated into Greek for the use of Greek-speaking Jews living in Egypt sometime after 132 B.C. (see the Prologue to the book). Only portions of the Hebrew text of the book have survived since it formed no past of the Hebrew canon. Five fragments of the Hebrew text were recovered from the Genizah (a depository for sacred texts) of a synagogue in Old Cairo in 1896 and following. Since then, a few verses of the text in Hebrew have been discovered among the Dead Sea (or Qumran) Scrolls.

The author of the book lived in Jerusalem (in chapter 50 he described how thrilling it was to watch the high priest Simon perform the liturgy in the Jerusalem temple). He was a schoolteacher who invited the untaught to come and lodge in his school (51:23). His book, a combination of proverbial wisdom (like the book of Proverbs) and rudimentary philosophy, was written before the wars between the Jews and the Seleucid Greeks created turmoil in Palestine beginning in the mid-170s B.C. (see I and II Maccabees).

In this Sunday's lection, wisdom is the central topic. Just as the Prologue to the Gospel of John speaks of the Word (the *logos*) so Sirach speaks of Wisdom (*sophia*). Unlike the *logos*, which is described as masculine in gender and became incarnate in Jesus, *sophia* is feminine in depiction and comes to reside in Israel and Jerusalem. (Later *sophia* was identified with the Jewish law.) The tendency to describe wisdom as feminine, even alluring and seductive, is already found in the book of Proverbs (see Proverbs 8, which closely parallels Ecclesiasticus 24).

In 24:1-7, *sophia* or wisdom describes herself as what might be called universal reason, cosmic order, or the sense of existence. She describes herself as the direct product of the divine, having been immediately spoken into existence (verse 3*a*). Her presence is universal, prevading all things (verses 3*b*-6*a*) and being found among all people (verses 6*b*-7). Here, the Hebrew philosopher asserts that the special knowledge possessed by Israel, what may be associated with what Christians call "special revelation," is shared with all other people. All people possess a limited but true knowledge, true wisdom, a knowledge of the divine and the way the world really is.

In verse 8 following, wisdom declares that God ordered her to dwell in Israel and to take up residence in Jerusalem. (Some of the rabbis taught that the law sought to reside with many nations but was refused a dwelling place until Israel was willing to receive the divine Torah.) Among Israel, wisdom took root and grew. In verses 12-17, various plants are used to describe this growth, all emphasizing the luxuriance and beauty of the growth.

Psalm 147:12-20

The ancient Greek translation of the Old Testament (the so-called Septuagint) treated Psalm 147 as two psalms. Verses 1-11 were counted as Psalm 146 and verses 12-20 as Psalm 147. (In this version, some psalms that were independent in the Hebrew version were combined and some psalms were separated. This explains the variation in enumeration.) In Catholic texts, this division is still observed.

Modern scholarship often assumes that Psalm 147 is composed of three independent compositions (verses 1-6,

7-11, and 12-20). The calls to praise in verses 1, 7, and 12 are taken as introducing new units. By merely assuming that the psalm repeats a similar structure three times, however, it is possible to understand the psalm as a single composition.

The lection for today calls on Jerusalem/Zion to offer praise to Yahweh and then offers a variety of reasons for such praise. A series of ten actions of God can be seen in the descriptions: (1) he strengthens the city's defense (13a), (2) he gives the city offspring (13b), (3) he establishes peace in its borders (14a), (4) he provides wheat for food (14b), (5) he addresses the world (15), (6) he gives snow (16a), (7) he scatters frost (16b), (8) he makes it sleet (17), (9) he sends forth his word and melts the ice, snow, frost, and sleet (18), and (10) he makes known his word (his law) to Israel (19).

As in the Prologue to the Gospel of John and the text from Ecclesiasticus 24, the word/wisdom is pictured taking up residence in or being revealed in a special way to Israel. Verse 20 affirms the uniqueness of this relationship and knowledge, something granted to no other nation.

Ephesians 1:3-6, 15-18

Like the Gospel lesson for today, Ephesians sets Christmas into a context much larger than Bethlehem, or Jerusalem, or even Rome. The Christ-event is placed in the eternal will of God.

Ephesians falls naturally in two parts: chapter 1–3 which are highly liturgical, consisting primarily of prayers, blessings, doxologies, benedictions, and creeds; and chapters 4–6 which draw the implications of chapters 1–3 for the faith, life, and work of the church. The portion for today's epistle consists of a blessing, a thanksgiving, and an intercessory prayer.

Verses 3-6 of chapter 1 are the opening lines of the blessing that extends through verse 10, and very likely through verse 14. Finding places to put periods in the English translation of a very long sentence in the Greek text is a difficult editorial decision. Ordinarily Paul follows the salutation of his letters (here verses 1-2) with a thanksgiving. Here there is a blessing, a eulogy, pronounced on God. This is common in

Jewish worship, as for example, in grace at meals: "Blessed art thou, O Lord, who gives bread to the hungry." In both Mark (14:22) and Matthew (26:26), the formula "took bread, blessed, and broke it" may mean that Jesus at the Last Supper took bread, blessed *God*, and broke the bread. To "bless" God is to praise and give thanks to God.

The writer is blessing God for what God has done which, in verses 3-6, consists of three sweeping acts. First, God has blessed us in Christ with every blessing in heavenly places (verse 3). Spatial distinctions are removed here (as also in 2:6; 3:15; 6:12) so as to give cosmic sweep to the affirmation of what God has done in Christ. Paul often joins heaven and earth in declarations of the lordship of Christ (Phil. 2:6-11; Col. 1:15-16; I Cor. 15:24-25; Rom. 8:37-39), but here the meaning is that Christ's church has become beneficiary of all the favor that fills God's dwelling place. In fact, the writer says a bit later, God has "raised us up with him [Christ], and made us sit with him in the heavenly places in Christ Jesus" (2:6).

Second, God chose us in Christ before the foundations of the world (verse 4). Among some Jewish and early Christian writers, speaking of what God did before creating the world was a way of affirming the certainty of God's purpose and promises. In other words, some things are firmly set in the good grace of God and are neither promoted nor voided by the contingencies and changes in this world and in history. In Matthew 25:34, Jesus says, "Come, O blessed of my Father, inherit the kingdom prepared for you from the foundation of the world." John 1:1-18 takes the reader back prior to creation, and Paul speaks of Christians being in the purposes of God both before and after the life of the world (Rom. 8:28-30). A later Christian writing, *The Shepherd of Hermas,* also spoke of the church as existing before the world began. One can hardly think of a more impressive way of affirming the assurance of God's promise in spite of everything.

And finally, verse 5 says much the same thing but in a different way: God destined (designated ahead of time) us in love to be God's children, exhibits of God's freely bestowed grace in Christ (verse 6). From the beginning until the end there operates in and through the creation the certain purpose and will of God. Life does not have at its center caprice or lawlessness, nor is the will of God dark and vindictive. Rather God's plan for us is to be described with words such as grace, love, blessing, and chosen to be God's children.

The second part of our text, verses 15-18 (a strong case can be made for including verse 19), consists of a thanksgiving and a prayer of intercession. As stated earlier, thanksgivings are common to Paul's letters, but usually they occur immediately after the salutation. Some scholars believe the different pattern to this letter is one indication that Ephesians is the work of a follower and admirer of Paul. Certainly the letter does not carry the intimacy and warmth of Paul's letter to his other churches. For example, notice the distance in "I have heard of your faith" (1:15) and "assuming . . . you have heard of the stewardship of God's grace that was given to me" (3:2). But most certainly Pauline is the expression of thanks for his readers and the remembrance of them in his prayers (verse 16; Phil. 1:1-11; Rom. 1:8-10). Likewise Pauline is the prayer that the believers have the gifts of insight and discernment into the immensity of God's plan, God's grace, and God's empowering through the Holy Spirit (verses 17-19; Phil. 1:9; I Cor. 12:10). We live, of course, in this world of concrete, particular, and immediate needs, problems, and goals. It is vital, however, that we step back now and then and get some sense of the grander context of God's way in the world, a way marked by grace, love, hope, and the power of the Spirit.

John 1:1-18

The Prologue to the Gospel of John is always the Gospel lesson for the Second Sunday After Christmas. Appropriate as this is, the preacher will be aware that a major portion of the Prologue, verses 1-14, is always the Gospel for Christmas, Third Proper. And in Year B, additional use of this passage occurs on the Third Sunday of Advent in the treatment of John the Baptist's witness to Jesus (verses 6-8). All of this is testimony to the central place of John 1:1-18 in the church's faith and proclamation. There is enough here for all these services, and more, but the preacher, in planning the messages for Advent and Christmas, will want to be aware of the reappearances of this text in order to make full but not repetitive use of the witness of John's Prologue. Because comments on 1:1-14 can be found at Christmas, Third Proper, we will here attend to the remaining verses 15-18.

Verse 15 needs to be considered distinct from verses 16-18 because it is parenthetical to the literary form and principal subject matter of the Prologue. Verse 15 and verses 6-8 have been inserted by the writer into a hymn or poem about the Logos, the Word who became flesh. Extract these verses and the poetic quality of the passage is left undisturbed; in fact, it is restored to its uninterrupted flow.

After all, these verses are about John the Baptist. Then why are they here? They are included to say that John was not the Christ, the son of God (verses 6-8), but rather that he came to bear witness to Jesus (verse 15). The other Gospels tell us that John was of a priestly family of Judea (Luke 1:5-25), he dressed like the prophet Elijah (Mark 1:6), he preceded Jesus (Mark 1:2-4), he baptized Jesus (Mark 1:9), he made disciples (Mark 2:18), and he suffered a martyr's death (Mark 6:14-29). These are strong credentials for gaining popular favor. In fact, the Fourth Evangelist reports that even among religious leaders there was speculation as to whether John was the Christ (1:19-23). Little wonder, then, that the writer of our text places in a hymn to Christ two insertions telling the reader, "I am referring to Jesus, not to John." In the Synoptics, John never publicly identifies Jesus as the one who was to come, but in the Fourth Gospel, that Jesus is the Son of God is revealed to John (1:32-34) and John's ministry was to bear witness to Jesus (1:7-8, 15, 19, 32, 34). John was a strong and impressive figure. It is not easy for such persons to witness to the greatness of another, and it is not easy for the audience to look beyond him to the One to whom he bears witness. Many ministers of striking and attractive qualities can comment on how a messenger can easily hinder a message.

The other major theme in verses 15-18 not previously treated in commenting on verses 1-14 is that of "grace and truth." The phrase occurred in verse 14 and is repeated at verse 17. Of the two terms, "truth" is the one that continues throughout the Gospel. In contrast to what is only apparent and, therefore, false, this Gospel focuses on the true: the true light (1:9), the true God (3:33), the true worshipers (4:23), the true witness (5:31), the true bread (6:32), the true vine (15:1). Likewise Jesus is the truth (14:6), God's word is truth (17:17), the Holy Spirit is the Spirit of truth (16:13), and those who worship God are to worship in spirit and in truth (4:23). According to John's Gospel, Jesus came to reveal the truth: the truth about God, about the world, and about ourselves. Those who are of the truth and who would live the truth are drawn to Jesus (3:21; 18:37).

But what about "grace"? The fact is, the word occurs in this Gospel only in the Prologue, in verses 14, 16-17. Does grace, then, not appear in the Gospel once the narrative about Jesus begins at 1:19? Of course it does, even though the word does not. However, to see grace operative in this Gospel it is necessary to rid oneself of any notion that grace is permissiveness, or low demand, or getting off easy, or casual forgiveness. Grace is not the soft underside of God. Grace is the free expression of God's favor on whomever, wherever, apart from any human claims or merit. With this in mind, to find grace one has but to read the stories of Jesus at the wedding feast (2:1-11), with Nicodemus (3:1-15), with the woman of Samaria (4:1-42), with the official from Capernaum (4:46-53), with the invalid at the pool (5:1-16), with the hungry crowds (6:1-14), with the man born blind (9:1-38), with the sisters of the deceased Lazarus (11:1-44). Some may object that grace is not to be found in these stories; after all, they are not stories of Jesus' response to requests or pleas for help. True: they are not accounts of Jesus' *responses;* they are rather accounts of his *initiative,* choosing to bless, to heal, to feed, to restore. After all, is that not what grace is, the divine initiative, not the divine response? In this Gospel, Jesus is the incarnation of God's grace.

Epiphany

Isaiah 60:1-6; Psalm 72:1-14; Ephesians 3:1-12;
Matthew 2:1-12

Matthew's story of the visit of the Magi is the central text for Epiphany which is the time for commemorating the presentation of Christ to the world. The wealth and power of the nations pay homage to the king. Undoubtedly one text inspiring Matthew's story was Isaiah 60. Psalm 72, a psalm for a coronation, sustains the royal and triumphant language and was taken by early Christians as applying immediately to Israel's royalty but ultimately to "him who was born king of the Jews." Ephesians 3, while not employing the language of royalty, does affirm that Christ's presentation to the world certainly means the inclusion of all nations in God's purpose through the church.

Isaiah 60:1-6

This text has long held pride of place in the Advent-Epiphany Season. Its vivid imagery and dramatic language are echoed throughout the Christmas story.

These verses began a three-chapter section in Isaiah (60–62) characterized by the unconditional proclamation of salvation. These chapters contrast drastically with the preceding section (56–59) made up of calls to repentance, strong judgments, scathing warnings, and conditional promises. This shift in emphasis has often been taken as evidence that two different authors wrote the two different sections. Probably nothing more is involved than the prophet's sudden shift to the proclamation of God's unconditional mercy for reasons now unknown.

Three special emphases are found in this text which can be related to Epiphany. First of all, there is the call to Zion to arise and shine coupled with the promise that the glory of God has arisen over the people. Although darkness may cover the earth and its peoples, Zion will shine forth because of the revelation of the glory of Yahweh.

Second, the scattered exiles will return home (verse 4). This motif—the gathering of the scattered, the return of the exiles—is a common theme that one finds throughout the Old Testament but especially in the prophets. From the time Israel and Judah became caught up in the maelstrom of Near Eastern politics—beginning in the ninth century B.C.—her citizens were carried away to foreign lands. Palestine was located between Asia to the north, with its civilization centers in Mesopotamia between the Euphrates and Tigris Rivers, and Egypt to the south, with its magnificent cities nestled along the banks of the Nile. Thus the land of Palestine formed a coastal bridge joining two continents with desert to the east and the sea to the west. Wars between these two civilization centers always carried foreign armies through the Israelite homeland. When such wars raged and Israel and Judah became involved, aged parents watched their youth carried away to foreign lands as booty. The hope of the return of those exiled was passed down through history from one generation to another. The prophet here promises the reversal of this old course of history: "Your sons shall come from far, and your daughters shall be carried in the arms." The sight of the returning exiles streaming home is pictured making the city itself radiant and rejoiceful (verse 5a).

Third, not only would the native exiles return but also other nations, foreigners, and their kings would be attracted and come to Zion (verses 3, 5b-6). In the process, the wealth of the nations would flow to poverty-stricken Zion. The universal aspect of this latter movement is indicated by the geographical references to the sea (the West) and the Arabian kingdoms of the desert (the East). The prophet depicts the wealth of the sea and the exotic exports of the East (gold and frankincense) coming to Zion. Such heavy-laden camel caravans from the East would proclaim the praise of the Lord.

The content of this promise and proclamation of salvation must have been in Matthew's mind when he wrote the story of the visit of the Magi who came to Jerusalem because they had beheld his light in the East. Both this passage of Isaiah and that from Matthew give expression to the significant role that Israel and Jerusalem-Zion had long seen not only as their goal but their destiny—to be a light to the nations (see Isa. 2:1-4; 42:6).

Psalm 72:1-14

This psalm, which probably was a petitionary prayer of the community employed at the coronation of a king, requests the fulfillment of the aspirations associated with the Davidic monarchs. Like other royal psalms (see 2; 110), this psalm was written to honor the human king on his accession to the throne but was kept alive even after native kingship had ceased after the fall of Jerusalem. In their preservation and later liturgical use, such psalms were interpreted with reference to the messianic king who would come in the future. The Advent Season for Christians is the time when we confess that the messianic promises witnessed their fulfillment in the birth of the Christ Child.

Verses 8-11 and 15-17 of this psalm embody the central affirmation that finds expression in Epiphany, the manifestation of Jesus to the world. Any legitimate preaching on this text, however, should make clear that the sentiments it contains were first applied to actual Davidic rulers, then reinterpreted in terms of the Messiah to come, and finally applied to the birth and epiphany of Jesus.

Although a prayer, this text, like many prayers contains a lot of preaching, that is, it reminds the ruler of the responsibilities of the royal office. This can be seen in an analysis of the psalm.

This psalm gives expression not only to the status of the king amid the external world of the nations but also to the aspirations and hopes of the people for their benefit through the rule of the king. In addition, the psalm stresses the internal function of the king within Hebrew society.

The psalm opens with a prayer that the king would be given justice and righteousness so that his rule would establish a proper social order which was both just and prosperous (verses 1-4). The king is here presented as the guarantor of the social order responsible for the operation of justice in the community. As the defender of justice, the king bore a special obligation for the defense of the poor and needy against those who would oppress them.

The close association between the nation's well-being, health, and prosperity and the life and fate of the king appears throughout this psalm. Prayer is made for a long life for the king (verse 5) and for his reign to fall upon the nation like the showers and rain that fall upon the land, rejuvenating the crops (verse 6). Righteousness and peace, which are requested in verse 7, denote the existence of right conditions and the total well-being of the community.

The universal dominion of the Davidic ruler is the theme of verses 8-11. The mythological expressions, "from sea to sea" and "from the River to the ends of the earth" are equivalent to saying, "the whole world." "The kings of Tarshish and of the isles" were the Mediterranean powers to the west, and Sheba and Seba were the spice- and incense-rich states of South Arabia to the east. Both mythological and historical-geographical references are employed to give comprehensive expression to the universality of the dominion claimed by the Davidic king. The plea to God was that the king would have universal dominion over nations that would be submissive to his rule and lavish in their payment of tribute.

The responsibility of the king to protect and defend the weak members of society is the theme of verses 12-14. There were no laws in ancient Israel requiring the king to protect the rights of those members of society who were open to exploitation by the privileged, wealthy, and oppressive. In fact the Old Testament legal material dealing with the king is very limited. The only regulations are found in Deuteronomy 17:14-20. Nonetheless, the society placed the king under the moral obligation to defend the defenseless, to aid the needy, and to pity the weak. In fact, the prophets applied this moral imperative to the whole of Israelite society, demanding justice in social affairs as service to God (see Amos 5:10-15, 24; Isa. 1:12-23). The treatment of the poor, the fatherless, the widows, and the needy was seen as the real test of a society's commitment to divine justice. When the prophet Jeremiah wished to condemn the wicked King Jehoiakim, he did so by pointing to his construction of a lavish palace at the expense of the rights of the common man. When he wished to praise the good works of the righteous King Josiah, he did so by noting that this king "judged the cause of the poor and needy" (Jer. 22:13-17).

Ephesians 3:1-12

As early as the fourth century, Epiphany was celebrated in the Western Church as a way of commemorating the manifestation of Christ to the Gentiles. Just as the story of the Magi in today's Gospel reading provides in narrative form excellent symbolism for the universal impact of Christ's coming, so does this vital theme of the inclusion of the Gentiles within the church form the central theme of the epistolary text.

Even though the text is generally regarded as pseudo-Pauline, it belongs within the Pauline trajectory of early Christian traditions. The language and imagery are reminiscent of the genuine Pauline Letters where Paul uses the term "mystery" not only of the whole Christ-saga (I Cor. 2:1-13), but also with specific reference to the role of the Gentiles in salvation history (Rom. 9:25). Even so, the term itself is rare in the genuine Pauline Letters, and it becomes far more fully expanded in the Deutero-Pauline Letters (cf. e.g., Rom. 16:25-27). In these later Pauline Letters, especially in Ephesians, the "mystery hidden from the ages" has as its content the message that the Gentiles have been included as part of God's "new humanity." The mystery of Christ revealed to Paul is that "the Gentiles are fellow heirs, members of the same body, and partakers of the promise in Christ Jesus through the gospel" (verse 6; cf. Eph. 1:19; Col. 1:26-27; 2:2).

Several features of this text are worth noting in this understanding of the Epiphany celebration. First, the inclusion of the Gentiles was part of the initial intention of God: "the plan of the mystery [was] hidden for ages in God" (verse 9). The final unveiling of the mystery came late, but this course of events was part of the "eternal purpose" (verse 11) which was finally realized in Christ.

Second, the inclusion of the Gentiles was an event of truly cosmic significance. Typical of the letter to the Ephesians is the cosmic scale on which the purposes of God are sketched. "The principalities and powers in the heavenly places" (verse 10) are said to be witnesses to this unfolding of God's church, "the manifold wisdom of God." It is the church universal, not the church local, that is in view in Ephesians. The world view that is presupposed here is, of course, heavily indebted to Jewish apocalyptic (cf. Eph. 6:10-20), but in the author's time this was not only indigenous to Judeo-Christian thought, but provided one of the most effective sets of symbols through which he could express the universal and cosmic dimensions of the Christ-event.

What it means for the church to be genuinely ecumenical in the sense of our text—Christ's church as the one body in which hostility, alienation, and exclusivism among human beings is absent—is still an unrealized vision. The deeply rooted tradition of celebrating the universality of Christ's manifestation at Epiphany can serve as one more moment in the church's life where the people of God are called into account by the Word of God. Today's text warns us not to narrow this biblical vision of the universal church into a national, racial, regional, or even confessional church.

If one wishes to develop this text in this direction, it is possible to appeal to the same warrant in calling for a truly ecumenical church, namely, that it has been God's eternal purpose for there to be "one humanity" in Christ. Today, however, now that the church is essentially Gentile, our task is not to get Jewish Christians to make room for Gentiles, but to get Gentile Christians to make room for Jews. The Jewish-Christian aspect of the modern ecumenical debate has begun to confront squarely some of the issues facing the church as it seeks to define itself and its mission over against other peoples of God, most notably Jews. An abundant literature has begun to be generated and provides excellent resources through which Christian ministers can rethink and clarify their own position even as they invite their churches to become part of this critical reappraisal.

Matthew 2:1-12

Epiphany provides the preacher the occasion for sharing some of the grandest texts of the Bible, for this is the season to declare the manifestation of the divine Son. The revelation is no longer a baby in a manger, no longer a whisper in Bethlehem, but a voice from heaven at Jesus' baptism and the dazzling light of the Transfiguration. Epiphany begins, however, with an even earlier announcement of the glory of the Son of God, the visit of the Magi to Bethlehem (Matt. 2:1-12).

Matthew 2:1-12 is not a birth story. Matthew's birth account is in 1:18-25 and to that story 2:1-12 is not directly tied. "Now when Jesus was born in Bethlehem of Judea in the days of Herod the king" is a chronological introduction to the cycle of four stories extending through 2:23. These texts are properly treated quite apart from Luke's Nativity; trying to conflate Matthew and Luke is more confusing than helpful. The move to Matthew means a shift in the writer's purposes and the theological statements. The shift is dramatic: exit shepherds, enter Wise Men; exit stables, enter palace; exit poverty, enter wealth; exit angels, enter dreams; exit Mary's lullaby, enter Rachel's wail.

Our text, then, is better understood as an announcement story. The emphases in the story are three. First, Christ appears not for Israel alone but for the world. The Wise Men, neither named nor numbered, are probably astrologers and represent for Matthew the fulfillment of Isaiah 60:1-6 which prophesies the pilgrimage of the rulers of the nations to Jerusalem to worship Israel's God, bringing him gifts of gold and frankincense. The appearance of the light of God's glory initiates the era of universal worship. In addition, Numbers 24:17 speaks of a star arising out of Jacob, as does the Testament of Levi (18:3). Likewise, Hellenistic literature was not without its stories of heavenly configurations announcing events of great importance. There were available to Matthew and his readers quite sufficient resources for making his declaration that Christ is for the world, to be worshiped by all nations. This Gospel, known for its Jewishness, must not be misunderstood: statements of the universality of the Gospel are frequent (4:15-16; 25:31-46; 28:18-20). In fact, there is not a Gospel which will provide a supporting text for those who wish to be exclusive with reference to race, nationality, or sex.

A second emphasis in Matthew 2:1-12 is that Jesus Christ is the true king of Israel. To develop this theme Matthew uses Bethlehem (Mic. 5:2) and David (II Sam. 5:2) materials from the Hebrew Scriptures. One might wonder why the Davidic theme would be developed when it was potentially so troublesome, creating messianic expectations that would obstruct the purposes of Jesus' ministry (22:41-46). However, Matthew not only wishes to establish that Jesus is the royal shepherd of Israel (10:6; 15:24), but that his life and work were sufficiently witnessed in Israel's Scriptures to make rejection of him inexcusable.

A third and final emphasis in today's Gospel lesson is the hostility to Jesus and the gospel by the political and religious establishment. The tension is posed early in the account by the references to Herod the king and Jesus the king. To develop this theme, Matthew uses the account of the children (Exod. 2). Stories of old rulers being threatened by the birth of heirs to the throne were common in Matthew's day, but clearly the direct antecedent was the Moses story. This image of a tyrant, jealous and intimidated, screaming death warrants and releasing the sword of government against the innocent to preserve entrenched power stabs awake the reader and abruptly ends a quiet Lukan Christmas. But Matthew must speak the truth: Good News has its enemies. One has but to love to arouse hatred, but to speak the truth to strengthen the network of lies and deception. It is no mystery why One who gave himself to loving the poor and neglected of the earth would be killed; there are institutions and persons who have other plans for the poor and neglected. Of course, no one wants a hassle, much less a clash, but what shall Jesus' followers say and do? The fearful whisper, "Tell the Wise Men to be quiet about the Child."

Baptism of the Lord (First Sunday After Epiphany)

Genesis 1:1-5; Psalm 29; Acts 19:1-7;
Mark 1:4-11

If baptism is understood as a new beginning, then it is appropriate to look to Genesis 1 as background and perhaps as a source for analogies. Psalm 29, with its vivid portrayal of the union of natural storms with the voice and activity of God, moves the reader closer to the account of Jesus' baptism in Mark 1. That occasion was also one of disturbances in nature as well as a heavenly voice. Acts 19, which serves as the epistle for the day, raises again the thorny issues of John's baptism and the reasons why Jesus submitted himself to it.

Genesis 1:1-5

The selection of this text to be associated with the baptism of Jesus is based on considerations of both imagery and theology. The image of the Spirit of God moving over the waters, God speaking and thus creating, and the reference to the first day or day one remind us, at least in the way of analogies, of many features associated with the baptism of Jesus. Theologically, baptism as new creation can be seen against the original creation. Just as the original act of God inaugurated the first creation so the baptism of Jesus inaugurated his career and the baptism of individuals inaugurates their new creation.

When preaching from this text the minister should realize that its association with baptism is a secondary application made on the basis of imagery and theology and thus one should be willing to inform an audience of such secondary application.

In its primary emphasis and original intention, Genesis 1:1-5 proclaimed the Divine as the creator and all that existed as the created. Thus the world of creation is seen as dependent on the creator and as living and sustained by the continuing power of the Divine.

Some particular features in the theology and content of the text should be noted: (1) the text seems to presuppose that God's primary act is one of formation rather than creation; God gives shape and order to the earth which existed "without form and void"; out of chaos, God acts and speaks to produce cosmos; (2) the Spirit of God, as in baptism, is given its role to play in the inauguration of creation; (3) the speaking of God calls realities and new conditions into existence; (4) creation is a process of separation and thus the establishment of divinely ordained orders in the world; (5) creation involves naming and thus declaring and identifying that which God has called into being.

Psalm 29

This psalm was probably used in ancient Israelite worship as part of the fall festival which was also both a new year celebration and an occasion anticipating the coming autumn rains. Thus Psalm 29 describes the epiphany and action of God in terms of a storm. Some scholars have suggested that this psalm was borrowed by the Israelites from the Canaanites who first used it in connection with the worship of their god Baal who was the lord of weather and the storm.

The connection of the psalm with the baptism of Jesus is again very secondary and simply draws on some of the imagery of the psalm. The association is based primarily on the constant repetition of the expression, "the voice of the Lord," which also has associations with Jesus' baptism.

The primary emphasis in this psalm is the kingship and enthronement of God (see verse 10) which is demonstrated in the coming of the life-refreshing rainstorms on which the ancient Israelites depended. This description of the activity of God reflects the actual path taken by most Palestinian storms. The voice of the Lord (the thunder) upon the waters (verses 3-4) is reminiscent of the collecting storm clouds out over the Mediterranean Sea. The storm then moves into the

Phoenician coastal region with great ferocity causing the earth to reel and rock (verses 5-6). The storm moves southward with its flashing lightning shaking the wilderness of the desert (verses 7-8) and making the trees shake and tremble (verse 9). The response to God's action in the storm theophany is the response, "Glory," heard in the temple. With the storm as the action of God it is clear that the Divine sits enthroned over the chaos of the flood waters and is enthroned as king forever. The psalm concludes with a petition that God will strengthen and bless the people with peace (verse 11).

Just as the first storms and rainfall of the autumn made possible the beginning of a new planting and growing season, so the baptism of Jesus makes possible the beginning of new redemptive activity.

Acts 19:1-7

The true significance of the baptism administered by John the Baptist has always been something of an enigma. Was it a completely new practice without precedent, or was it analogous to the Jewish lustrations currently practiced in first-century Palestine? In looking at the Gospel account of Jesus' baptism, one can ask both historical and theological questions. From a historical perspective, one question is what it actually signified in terms of Jesus' own life and work. For example, it appears that submitting to John's baptism meant that Jesus himself became one of John's followers. At the theological level, one might ask about its significance in terms of Jesus' messianic status or self-understanding. In second-century Gnostic circles, the baptism of Jesus was regarded as the moment where he became "Son of God" in a real sense. Christ's Epiphany was closely identified with this event in his life. Or, the stress could fall on other moments in his life as the time or moment when his true divinity became manifest: his birth, his first miracle at Cana, his Transfiguration, or his resurrection. Thus, the baptism of Jesus came to be understood as an important moment in determining the point where Christ's divinity first became manifest.

One problem faced by the early church concerned the

reason Jesus was baptized by John. As this text from Acts indicates, and as the Gospels confirm, John's baptism was a "baptism of repentance" (verse 4). It required a change of heart and life which signified that the person who received such a washing was preparing for the last days. The Gospel accounts, however, also indicate that John saw himself as the messianic forerunner who pointed beyond himself to Jesus as God's designated Messiah. It was he who would truly usher in God's new age, the earmark of which would be the Holy Spirit. Consequently, Christian baptism as it was practiced in the early church was distinguished from John's baptism primarily in this respect: that it brought with it the gift of the Holy Spirit in a way John's baptism did not (Acts 2:38).

In Ephesus when Paul discovered these twelve disciples who had been members of John's movement, he asked them—to determine whether they were aware that the Messianic Age had dawned—if they had received the Holy Spirit. Clearly, they had not, and Paul responded by baptizing them "in the name of the Lord Jesus" (verse 5), after which, through the laying on of his hands, they received the Holy Spirit, spoke in tongues, and prophesied.

In the ancient church, in some areas, Epiphany was the time of the year when converts or catechumenates were baptized. Thus, Epiphany became an occasion for double celebration: for remembering the baptism of Jesus and for witnessing the incorporation of new members into the congregation. Accordingly, Epiphany can have a dual focus for Christian reflection and preaching as we think, first, of the significance of Jesus' own baptism, and, second, of our own. How central to Christian life and thought is the baptism of Jesus is attested by the popularity of this event in Christian art. As one reflects on the historical and theological significance of Jesus' own baptism, it becomes an appropriate time for one to reflect on the significance of one's own baptism. Similar issues of vocation arise: baptism as an expression of sonship with all the requisite obedience that it entails; repentance as both a point of departure and a continuous style of life for the one who has been incorporated into Christ through baptism; baptism as the time when one's life is intersected by the divine thrust of the Spirit of God who both signifies, calls to, and enables genuine sonship.

Several homiletical possibilities present themselves as one reflects on this passage from Acts 19:1-7 in the context of the celebration of the baptism of Jesus. First, the relationship between John the Baptist and Jesus as that of prophetic forerunner to the expected Messiah. Second, significant elements of the baptismal rite which prompt Christian reflection, such as repentance and the Spirit as God's gift to baptized believers. Third, the Holy Spirit as the certifying agent of genuine Christian conversion and the ways in which this can manifest itself in the contemporary church.

Mark 1:4-11

For those with the historian's mind in search of the facts about Jesus' life, the baptism of Jesus provides a certainty. This conclusion does not follow because all three Synoptics record it but because Jesus' being baptized came to be problematic for the church. Why would the Christ, the Son of God be baptized? Matthew is sensitive to the problem as reflected in John's hesitancy to baptize Jesus (3:14), while Luke, without mentioning who baptized Jesus, joins baptism and prayer in a subordinate clause, giving primary attention to the divine witness to Jesus (3:21-22). Later Christian documents glorified the entire scene with bright light and fire over the surface of the water. For Mark, the baptism of Jesus is an epiphany, but the brief account reflects no tension nor does it carry side arguments aimed at detractors. Mark apparently was confident his readers understood that among the baptisms by John, that of Jesus was unique.

Even though our text for today is Mark 1:4-11 we will give attention only to verses 9-11 because this is the account of the baptism proper and because verses 1-8 were discussed in the material for the Second Sunday in Advent. The baptism of Jesus is the second of the three parts of Mark's introduction: the ministry of John (verses 1-8), the baptism of Jesus (verses 9-11), and the temptation of Jesus (verses 12-13). Mark states clearly and briefly that Jesus was baptized by John in the

Jordan, but in an accent characteristically Markan, Jesus is identified as a Galilean from Nazareth (1:9; 1:24; 10:47; 14:67; 16:6). Galilee, not Judea, is home and even after the resurrection, Jesus' disciples were to meet him in Galilee (16:7). Also in Mark, the heavens splitting, the Spirit descending, and the voice from heaven are seen and heard by Jesus alone. The event does not carry, as does Matthew 3:16-17, any public declaration about Jesus. Only Jesus and the reader receive heaven's testimony.

Mark's message here is threefold. First, Jesus' baptism and the beginning of his public life usher in the new age, the eschatological time. The signs are the splitting of the heavens (Isa. 64:1; Ezek. 1:1), the descent of the Spirit (Isa. 11:2; 42:1; 61:1-4), and the voice from heaven (Ps. 2:6-7; Isa. 42:1). The one mightier than John who would baptize with the Holy Spirit (1:7-8) is here. The plan of God and the experience of Mark and the church join in the testimony that Jesus means a new age. Mark's second message is that Jesus is declared Son of God. Mark has already said so (1:1) and will again (9:2-8; 15:39), but here the expression, which can have any number of meanings (for example, Adam is called son of God, Luke 3:38), is given specific content. The message of the voice from heaven combines Psalm 2:7, which is God's declaration of sonship at the coronation of a king, and Isaiah 42:1, a portion of a description of the Servant of the Lord. By the union of these two very different texts, Jesus as Son of God is portrayed both sovereign and servant. This is to state in part the third of Mark's emphases in this brief text: the commissioning of Jesus for ministry. In his work Jesus will be mightier than John, for in the power of the Holy Spirit he will do battle against demons and all the evil forces that maim, cripple, alienate, and destroy human life. But in him will be no arrogant display of power, for he is the Servant of God whose ministry will take him to the cross.

It is clear, even in Mark's brief record, that the baptism of Jesus was not only epiphany, a declaration of the Son of God, but was also, by Mark's time, a statement of the church's self-understanding. The church understood that as disciples of Jesus, they were people of the new age. They also had come to associate baptism with the Holy Spirit, a connection apparently widespread in the early church (Acts 2:38; 19:1-7). As the people of the new age they shared that power made available through Jesus Christ, the Holy Spirit. For all the varieties of interpretations of the Holy Spirit, this gift was the hallmark of the Christian movement. And finally, the church had come to associate baptism and the commission to serve. By baptism the whole church was called to ministry, the recollection of baptismal vows functioning as a kind of ordination. If Jesus was designated Servant of God and declared concerning himself that he "came not to be served but to serve" (Mark 10:45), then one definition of discipleship was and is unavoidably clear.

Second Sunday After Epiphany

I Samuel 3:1-10 (11-20); Psalm 63:1-8; I Corinthians 6:12-20;
John 1:35-42

Last Sunday's lections centered on the baptism of Jesus and its implications for Christian baptism. Today we are moved beyond baptism to the life that follows it. The reading from First Samuel relates the call to service that Samuel received. Psalm 63 is an expression of trust in God in a relationship that never leaves the psalmist's mind, even during the night hours. The moral implications of the life of discipleship, or as Paul says, "in Christ," are spelled out in I Corinthians 6. The Gospel text presents the witness to Christ by John the Baptist. Those who hear are offered the invitation to trust, to "come and see." Trust responds by "abiding" with him.

I Samuel 3:1-10 (11-20)

This lection constitutes what might be designated either the infancy narrative about the prophet Samuel or the account of his call into the service of prophecy by God. How Samuel had been conceived by the barren Hannah as a child of promise is told in I Samuel 1. As a response to the gift of a child, the mother presented Samuel to the service of God at the temple in Shiloh then under the care and service of the old priest Eli and his disappointingly decadent sons (see I Sam. 2:12-17).

Samuel served in the Shiloh temple under Eli's supervision from the time of his weaning. (Hebrew children were weaned at about the age of two or three years.) His early service was obviously that of a mere functionary during these days since he "did not yet know the Lord, and the word of the Lord had not yet been revealed to him" (3:7).

Several points are made in this narrative about Samuel, his call, and his message.

1. Samuel's nocturnal call by God was met by an enthusiastic response on the part of the lad. The fact that God calls three times without the source of the call being recognized, that Samuel thinks it is Eli, and that the priest only slowly realizes that it might be God speaking to the lad are all dramatic touches in the story. They are not intended to condemn Eli so much as to illustrate the point made in the opening verse: "The word of the Lord was rare in those days; there was no frequent vision." The fact that religion had reached this point made the old priest, now with eyesight so dim he could not see (another dramatic touch), unexpectant about any word or vision from God. Samuel, even though he does not realize the source of the voice addressing him, responds vigorously offering himself to the priest with a hearty, "Here I am" (see Isa. 6:8). Once the source of the voice is known, in God's fourth call, Samuel responds with a promise of a faithful hearing: "Speak, for thy servant hears" (verse 10).

2. The call of Samuel is the inauguration of a new state of affairs in Israel and Shiloh. God announces to the youngster that a new thing is about to be done which will startle everyone when they hear it (verse 11). Thus the prophet becomes the confidant of God, the sharer in the divine determination of events, and the spokesperson of what is about to dawn.

3. The word of God about the future is a word of judgment, a word condemning the house of Eli, and it is Samuel who must be the bearer of the word to those under whose service he has labored (verses 12-18).

4. The inauguration of Samuel's career was followed by a stage of service in which "the Lord was with him and let none of his words fall to the ground" (verse 19). The fidelity of the prophet involved the hearing and the proclamation of the word even when the word was one of judgment on his own people and co-laborers. God supported the work of Samuel by seeing that none of his words fell unfulfilled.

5. Samuel's activity and proclamation established his reputation as a prophet throughout Israel—"from Dan to

Beer-sheba"—so that his work brought a reversal of affairs in Israel (compare verse 20 with verse 1). Where vision and word had been rare they now became frequent.

This text has been selected for the Season of Epiphany to illustrate the typological correspondences between Samuel's call and response and his nurture in the Lord and those of Jesus (see Luke 2:52). Like Samuel, Jesus is called and designated as an eschatological prophet to his own people with a message that will establish his reputation and ultimately strike at the temple itself.

Psalm 63:1-8

This psalm contains some features of a lament but in a lament that expresses great trust and confidence in God. Some of its imagery correlates with that of the Samuel narrative. Verse 2 reminds one of Samuel's service in the sanctuary (I Sam. 3:3) and the reference to his thinking of God when he was in bed and meditating on God in the watches of the night (verse 6) recall the nocturnal character of Samuel's call (I Sam. 3:15).

The lament character of the psalm is indicated by its consistent address to the Deity and by the strong expression of longing for God (see the opening verse especially). The worshiper desires most of all a compassionate communion and fellowship with God or the continuation of such a relationship. The images of seeking, thirsting, and fainting for God may be compared with the eagerness with which Samuel responded to the word of God. The dry and weary land without God recalls the Israel of Samuel's day when the infrequent presence of God was an accepted and common phenomenon (I Sam. 3:1).

Like most laments, this psalm contains a vow or promise of future action. In verses 3-4, the psalmist promises that her/his lips will praise God and that God will be the object of the petitioner's worship for the rest of life.

The final four verses of the lection are a statement of absolute trust and confidence probably based on the experience of worship noted in verse 2. Numerous images are detailed to express this trust and confidence. The soul is satisfied like one who has feasted on bone marrow and fat. Even when lying upon the bed and thinking of God through the watches of the night, when one is most apt to be aware of life's true relationships and tormented by troubles and conscience, there is still confidence. God has been so much of a help that the petitioner, now turned thanksgiver, can describe the human-divine relationship as being under protective wings like a baby bird protected by its mother.

Finally, the psalmist emphasizes the mutuality of the divine-human relationship. The worshiper clings to God, and God's right hand, the hand of strength, upholds the worshiper.

I Corinthians 6:12-20

"Shun [sexual] immorality" (verse 18) aptly states the gist of Paul's exhortation here. Within the young Corinthian church an elite minority of its members were pushing the Pauline theme of "freedom in Christ" beyond its limits. Paul begins by quoting their own slogans: "All things are lawful for me" (verse 12) and "food is meant for the stomach and the stomach for food" (verse 13). The one expresses their permissive, libertine outlook, the other their insistence that eating is a physical act, nothing more.

By extension, they apparently contended that they had similar license in sexual matters (cf. I Cor. 5:1-2; 15:29-34). They could do as they wished with their bodies, they thought, since sexual intercourse, like eating, was a physical activity, nothing more. By making a sharp distinction between the spirit and the body, one could easily stress the importance of the former and the relative unimportance of the latter. One could nourish the spirit but do with the body whatever one pleased, confident that the one did not affect the other.

In response, Paul first insists that "freedom" as the Corinthian gnostics understood it, is an illusion, for it not only produces behavior that is "not helpful," either to the individual or to the group (cf. I Cor. 8), but also produces the opposite effect—it actually results in "enslavement" (verse 12). Moreover, such a schizophrenic view of the human personality ignores God's sovereignty over all things—spirit and body. The body, by which Paul understands the whole human personality, far from being "merely physical," is "for the Lord," that is, the risen Lord. Thus Christian existence is only properly understood when defined by the risen Lord; in fact, the "Lord [is] for the body" (verse 13), probably in the sense that the redemptive work of Christ was after all directed toward the individual: "You were bought with a price" (verse 20). The body can hardly be ill esteemed if one considers the full import of the resurrection: just as the Lord was raised so will all those who have been incorporated into Christ. Our destiny, indissolubly linked with Christ's, involves the whole human personality—"the body."

Another line of response is Paul's reminder of the corporate dimension of Christian existence (verses 15-20). Three times he uses the phrase, "Do you not know . . . ," to introduce his instructions. The formula is typically used to introduce familiar, traditional instruction. Thus the Corinthians are being called to remember that which they should have realized already. First, that being "in Christ" has corporate implications. What the Christian does with his or her body directly involves, if not implicates, the other members (verse 15). Second, sexual intercourse with one who has not been declared of "one flesh" according to the biblical understanding of marriage (Gen. 2:24), is not merely a "physical activity," but the creation of a new relationship involving the whole person. Union with the Lord results in being "one spirit with him" (verse 17), and this suggests that relationships involving persons with each other sexually are to be taken with the utmost seriousness because they extend to and involve the whole human personality. Entangling alliances are created even if one views the relation as casual, particularly when it involves sexual union. Third, the body is not to be understood as radically separate from spirit, but is to be understood as the very temple of God's Holy Spirit (verse 19). It can never be understood as anything other than a sanctuary serving as a dwelling place for God's own presence.

The cumulative effect of all these reminders is that those "in Christ" are not "their own" in any unqualified sense.

"Freedom in Christ" is precisely that: "in Christ." The way this phrase is used by Paul suggests that being incorporated with Christ indissolubly links the Christian with God, Christ, the Spirit, and the community of believers for whom these are all living realities. Individual behavior for those "in Christ" can never be individual per se, for it has theological, ecclesiological, and eschatological dimensions.

Paul's advice here is broadening rather than narrowing, for some Corinthians have viewed both themselves and their behavior in too restricted a sense. They are thus called to redefine their Christian perspective so that it encompasses the whole spectrum of existence "in Christ."

John 1:35-42

The biblical word central to the Season of Epiphany is "revelation," for this is the time to celebrate the revealing of the Son of God. But the companion word to revelation is "witness," for revelation in the biblical sense is never open and obvious to everyone, interested or not, believer or not. There is always about it a kind of radiant obscurity, a concealing that requires faith to grasp the revealing. One is not permitted a controlled, managed, guaranteed, no-risk response to Jesus. Those, therefore, who have beheld the glory become flesh (John 1:14) cannot prove, but they can witness. Witnessing to the revelation does not refer to lengthy self-disclosures, narrating one's feelings in response to the word, but rather to confession of what one has seen and heard. No one understands this better than the author of the Fourth Gospel who, after a prologue announcing the revelation (1:1-18), follows with a series of accounts of witnessing to Jesus Christ (1:19-51).

In the Gospel of John, witnessing to Christ begins with John the Baptist (1:29-34). Verses 19-28 are primarily John's witness about himself, that he is not the Christ. John's testimony causes two of his disciples to follow Jesus (verses 35-42), and they in turn witness to their friends (verses 43-51), creating an ever-widening circle of testimony, faith, and further testimony. It will be important for the preacher not to allow the Synoptic accounts of the relation of John and

Jesus to bleed into the text before us. While the Synoptics have Jesus beginning his ministry in Galilee after John is imprisoned, the Fourth Evangelist says both ministered in Judea, and at the same time (1:29–4:3). That Jesus' first disciples came to him from John with John's encouragement is vital to this Gospel's understanding of the nature and purpose of the Baptist's mission.

John 1:35-42 provides the reader with the content of the witness about Jesus in the Baptist's circle and the dynamic of that witness in the generation of faith. The content of John's testimony, "Behold, the Lamb of God" (verse 36), is one of the enigmas of the Gospel. Allusions from the Hebrew Scriptures are plentiful, in fact, too plentiful for the precise meaning here to be clear. There was the sin-offering lamb, the warrior lamb of apocalyptic literature, the Passover lamb, as well as lambs offered on other days of sacrifice. One might suppose the sin-offering was in mind here, especially in view of Jesus' saying he lays down his life for the sheep (10:11). However, the death of Jesus as an atonement is scarcely developed in this Gospel. When Jesus dies the imagery is that of a Passover lamb (19:31-37) whose death ends one kind of passover and initiates another. The preacher would do well to explore the rich variety of meanings in the image rather than tell the listeners with certainty what John had in mind.

By far the major attention of our text is given to the dynamic of witness in the generation of faith. Notice: John witnesses about Christ and points him out to two of his own disciples; they follow Jesus; Jesus asks what they are seeking; they desire to know where he is staying or abiding; he invites them to come and see; they abide with him; one of them finds his brother and witnesses to him. Three observations about this story are in order: first, the pattern is important in the Gospel. Briefly stated, they heard, they inquired, they experienced, they believed, they witnessed. Second, within this pattern the spoken word is very important, followed by an actual experience of Christ. These elements in the creation of faith will occur repeatedly in this Gospel. As two examples, recall the experiences of the Samaritans (4:28-42) and of Thomas (20:19-29). Witnessing is more than words, of course, but it is not less than words. Those who discount the value of spoken words are often seeking to avoid the most difficult of human endeavors: speaking appropriately about subjects profoundly important to both speaker and listener. Third, this brief narrative introduces us to the writer's call to faith and the response of faith that is deep and life-giving. The invitation, "Come and see," occurs throughout the Gospel (1:39; 1:46; 4:29; 11:34), indicating how faith is initiated and how it grows. The response "to stay" or "to abide" expresses the relationship to Christ that is of the kind that exists between Christ and God (1:38-39; 4:40; 14:2, 23; 15:4-11). In this Gospel, to abide in Christ is to have here and hereafter blended into one life, the life eternal.

Third Sunday After Epiphany

Jonah 3:1-5, 10; Psalm 62:5-12; I Corinthians 7:29-31 (32-35);
Mark 1:14-20

All the readings for this Sunday remind the preacher and the church that with the Epiphany of God, whether that takes the form of prophetic call, a prayerful reflection, a pastoral exhortation, or an encounter with the person of Jesus, there comes a radical shift in values and life orientation. Life does not continue the same. Jonah was the instrument of that change in Nineveh. Psalm 62 affirms trust in God and immediately recognizes the transient value of material goods. Paul reminds the Corinthian church that the surpassing worth of Christ relativizes all other values. And when fishermen are called by Jesus of Nazareth, Mark says they left everything behind.

Jonah 3:1-5, 10

The prophetic Book of Jonah differs from all the other prophetic books in that it is primarily a narrative with practically no prophetic proclamation. It is a story about a prophet, his reluctance to preach repentance to the hated Assyrians living in Nineveh, and his final submission to the prophetic task and the subsequent repentance of the Ninevites.

The Book of Jonah is thus best understood as a prophetic legend which has been built around the single reference to a prophet named Jonah who is said to have prophesied during the days of King Jeroboam II of Israel who reigned in the middle of the eighth century B.C. (II Kings 14:25). Jonah in the legend represents the staunch nationalistic, anti-universalistic attitude that seems to have characterized Israelite religion and outlook at times.

129

The first part of the book (chapters 1–2) presents the prophet in his futile and feverish attempt to escape the prophetic task placed on him. The story of the great fish, which so often occupies the attention of preachers to the exclusion of the second half of the book, occurs in this section. Jonah's attempt to escape his role and the fish story emphasize the persistence of God in seeing that the divinely appointed tasks are carried out.

Even on the occasion of the second call, Jonah still grudgingly hesitates to fulfill the obligations of the prophetic task. Eventually, however, he goes to Nineveh whose size is also described in legendary terms. (Excavations at the site of the ancient city have revealed a town about one and a half miles in diameter—not one that would require a three-day journey to cross.) When Job proclaims that Nineveh will be overthrown in forty days, the people believe God and manifest signs of remorse—fasting and wearing coarse-clothed garments ("sackcloth"). Both people and beasts share in the attitude (see 3:7-9).

Interestingly enough, it is not the citizens of Nineveh who repent but God (verse 10). For us moderns, references to God's repentance strike us as incompatible with the divine nature. The Old Testament, however, was quite willing to speak of the divine change of mind as in this text (see Amos 7:1-4).

This lection from Jonah presents him as a type or an antitype to Jesus. Jesus is said to have compared the Son of man (himself) to Jonah as a sign of the judgment of God. Unlike Jonah, Jesus appears as a willing proclaimer of the kingdom of God and judgment, but both are representative of the prophetic call to repentance.

Psalm 62:5-12

This reading has been selected for the lectionary because it manifests confidence and hope in God, the proper response to the call to both repentance and discipleship. In addition, the reading stresses the fact that God requites persons according to their work, that is, according to their obedience and the character of their discipleship.

The homiletician should realize that this section of the psalm has a very complicated structure in that it contains a confessional statement of the worshiper (verses 5-7), a call to others to trust in God (verse 8), proclamation about the delusive character of human wealth and prestige over against the power and stability of God (verses 9-11), and finally an address to the Deity which affirms God's fidelity both in love and in just rewards (verse 12).

The psalm exudes confidence in God who is described as a rock, salvation, a fortress, and a mighty rock, all images suggesting refuge and protection. Having such protection, especially against one's enemies and the slander of gossip (verses 3-4), allows the psalmist to possess hope and to pledge loyalty in spite of all circumstances.

This confidence theme can be better understood in light of the possible original usage of the psalm. The text sounds very much like psalms that were prayed in a temple ritual in which a person had been falsely accused. Whenever a court case or charge could not be proven because of lack of evidence or failure of the elders to reach a verdict, the parties could appeal their case to the temple priests and thus to God (see Exod. 22:7-8; Deut. 17:8-13; I Kings 8:31-32). The other party in this psalm seems to be referred to in verses 3-4. The parties in the case could express their confidence in the outcome by reciting such psalms as this one. Frequently the priests may have been able to determine if one was guilty or innocent of the charge. If they could not, then the parties could swear their innocence in an oath or self-imprecation. The confidence in this psalm suggests that the worshiper, although having been charged, was certain of his/her relationship to the Deity and that the charge was a falsehood (see verse 4). The worshipers with such certainty in their innocence could throw themselves upon the divine and claim the Deity as their place of refuge and the hope of their salvation.

The psalmist also denounces confidence in human status and wealth declaring low and high estates to be worthless when placed in the balances and weighed before God—"they are together lighter than a breath" (verse 9). Neither extortion nor robbery (do these reflect something of the charge brought against the psalmist?) is an object of hope, and riches should not be the object of one's ambitions. This suggests, in light of the preaching of repentance and the call to discipleship, that people must turn their back on everything humanly materialistic in order to confront and answer the call to be a true follower.

The minister can use verse 11 in the context of the Christian year and the exposition of Jesus' call of the disciples. The proclamation of God's power to fulfill the promises involved in the call to service has been heard, the psalmist declares, more than once and the message is always the same—"power belongs to God." Faithful hearing and following mean trusting in God's steadfast love and knowing that the task undertaken will be rewarded because God requites according to one's work (verse 12).

I Corinthians 7:29-31 (32-35)

The first question to be decided here is how far to extend the pericope. Strictly speaking, verses 29-31 are a self-contained unit, although the Revised Standard Version combines them with the paragraph begun in verse 25. The New English Bible and the Jerusalem Bible, however, conform to the latest edition of the Greek text and print them as a separate paragraph. Suffice it to say, if verses 29-31 are read without verses 32-35, the congregation, unless it is familiar with the context, will not know that these words occur in the very heart of Paul's extended treatment of the question of marriage in I Corinthians 7.

Verses 29-31 are crucial to Paul's remarks in the chapter as a whole for setting the eschatological framework in which his instructions are given. They make clear that the Corinthians' questions concerning marriage, about which they have written him (verse 1), were directly related to their eschatological expectations. Anxiety about the imminence of Christ's coming had widespread effects within the church. For those already married, it raised the question whether they should suspend or modify the normal demands of marriage (verses 1-7). The unmarried wondered whether they should enter new relationships which, by their very nature, would divert their attention from spiritual matters and preparation for the Parousia (verses 25-28, 32-35).

Broadly speaking, Paul's advice throughout the chapter is for the Corinthian Christians, whatever their marital status, to retain the status quo. Each group addressed within the chapter is advised to remain as it is, if at all possible, primarily because of the unsettling conditions expected to precede the eschaton. Such advice is eschatologically motivated: "the time we live in will not last long" (verse 29, NEB); "the world as we know it is passing away" (verse 31, JB). Here, of course, it is clear that Paul shares the early Christian expectation of the speedy return of the Lord (cf. I Cor. 16:22).

What is especially significant to notice about verses 29-31 is Paul's insistence that this overarching eschatological viewpoint relativizes the way in which we relate to ordinary human activities. Domestic priorities shift: "Those who have wives should live as though they had none" (verse 29, JB). Personal human emotions are no longer absolute: "those who mourn should live as though they had nothing to mourn for; those who are enjoying life should live as though there were nothing to laugh about" (verse 30, JB). Commercial and economic activity is likewise understood in a new way: "Those whose life is buying things should live as though they had nothing of their own" (verse 30b, JB). In short, one's stance toward "the world" is now redefined because God's purpose is much broader: "Those who have to deal with the world should not become engrossed in it" (verse 31, JB).

What Paul is calling for here is the same type of sober reevaluation that instinctively occurs when we face a genuine crisis, particularly one that is sudden and unexpected. If our child is suddenly struck with some mystifying paralysis, our whole life routine suddenly halts. What were previously pressing engagements immediately become postponable as we reorient ourselves to the truly life-demanding needs at hand. Nothing engages us in the same way until the crisis is met, and once it is over, there is inevitably the residual effect of the reevaluation. As we pick up were we left off, we usually do so resolving to live with a new set of priorities.

Viewed one way, Paul's remarks here are radically world-denying. They could easily be taken to mean that

Christians should suspend all normal activity as they prepare for Christ's return. That he was so misunderstood is clear, as is the fact that this is not what he meant (cf. II Thess. 3:6-13). The key phrase in verses 29-31 is "as if not" *(hos me)*. Ordinary activities continue as we await the Parousia: we continue to marry, weep, and rejoice, buy and sell, and deal with the world, but we do none of these "as if" they were ultimate ends in themselves. They are now seen as good and worthwhile activities of penultimate value. They are properly viewed when set within the context of the transitoriness of this age and properly valued when set over against a future that belongs ultimately to God. We can live "now" seriously but not obsessively; we can look forward to the "not yet" confidently, but not naïvely.

Mark 1:14-20

Before considering our text for today, three preliminary comments to the preacher might be helpful. First, if last Sunday's sermon was based on the Gospel lesson, John 1:35-42, then the listeners may need some help in handling the shift to Mark 1:14-20. According to Mark, Jesus began his ministry in Galilee, following John's imprisonment, and his first disciples were fishermen of Galilee. This would be an appropriate time to make brief but clear remarks about the integrity of each Gospel's purpose and perspective and the problems created by homogenizing them into one life of Jesus. Second, since today's lesson concerns the launching of Jesus' ministry, one will be tempted to draw much supporting and clarifying material from later chapters in Mark. However, Mark is the primary Gospel this year and many more occasions for messages from Mark will be provided. Rather than stealing from the future, why not do what Mark does? Invite the listeners to move with Jesus "on the way," asking and learning as they go. And third, let the fact that this is an Epiphany text be the magnet that gathers the several sub-themes that entice down sermonic side roads.

Mark 1:14-20 consists of two parts: verses 14-15 are pivotal, making transition from the introduction (verses 1-13) and providing a summary description of Jesus' public ministry; verses 16-20 give a concrete example of commitment to the word and work of Jesus. Having been tested by Satan and empowered by the Spirit (verses 12-13), Jesus begins his public ministry. By stating without explanation that John had been arrested, Mark assumes the reader knows what he himself will relate later (6:17-29). The first image of Jesus is that of preacher, one of Mark's three favorite portraits of him, teacher and exorcist being the other two. Jesus' message is that now is the fullness of time (Gal. 4:4), now is God's time and the kingdom of God is at hand. (It is impossible from word study alone to know whether "at hand" means "here" or "near." Both meanings are possible since the kingdom is both present and future according to the Gospels.) The background for the idea of God's kingdom or God's rule lies in Judaism. The reference is to the total reign of God (Isa. 52:7; Ps. 45:6; 103:19), whether through the processes of historical events or as a divine interruption of history. When history was so oppressive as to say no to the rule of God, hope remained tenacious and said yes to God's sovereign rule as an act from above, breaking in upon history. Those who heard Jesus' announcement of the presence of the kingdom were to repent of false assumptions and wrong-doing, turning toward God with full trust in the Good News.

The second unit of our lesson, verses 16-20, is a concrete case of believing response. Jesus preaches the gospel and calls for disciples. The story is so brief as to be called "telescoped"; that is, an event that may have transpired over a longer period is presented as swift and complete. The fact is, Mark gives no details as to what might have been telescoped, and the absence of details makes the story even more vivid. The call of these four disciples is a call of crisp radicality. Discipleship means leaving property and family, says Mark. In the words of Martin Luther, followers of Jesus "let goods and kindred go."

In order to achieve focus on Mark 1:14-20, one must ask, In what sense is this an Epiphany text? Several answers are possible, all related to the appearance of Jesus in public as preacher and caller of disciples. But not to be overlooked is the expression, "The time is fulfilled" (verse 15). In the New

Testament are two words for time. One is *chronos* from which we get chronology and which speaks of years and months and days, of calendars and clocks. The other word is *kairos* which calls attention to a special time, an opportune time, a time in which the constellation of factors creates an unusually significant moment. In the Fourth Gospel, Jesus speaks often of his "hour": his hour has not come, his hour has come, now is the hour to be glorified. Such is the sense of Mark 1:15. Whatever the year or month or day; wherever the place; whoever may be in control or under control; suddenly or slowly, noisily or quietly, God acts, Jesus appears, and it is *kairos*. In the reading from Jonah, Nineveh knew it; in the reading from First Corinthians, Paul knew it. In fact, everyone who hears and believes the Good News experiences this kind of time.

Fourth Sunday After Epiphany

*Deuteronomy 18:15-20; Psalm 111; I Corinthians 8:1-13;
Mark 1:21-28*

Today's lections present us with an array of ways God is among us, finally coming to expression in Jesus Christ. Psalm 111 recites the activities of God that Christians associate with the activities of Jesus. Deuteronomy 18 speaks of a prophet arising from among the people, a prophet Christians identified as Jesus. Paul writes to the Corinthians about the role of the living Christ in the church to create love, patience, unity, and humility. Finally, the Gospel of Mark presents Jesus in two roles not only prominent in Mark but sometimes joined as two aspects of one ministry: the teacher and the exorcist.

Deuteronomy 18:15-20

The Book of Deuteronomy, composed as Moses' farewell address to the Hebrews just before they moved across the Jordan River, outlined for the people the ways of obedience and warned against disobedience in their new life in the Land of Promise. The book was thus concerned with the future and the shape that the future would take.

One element in that future is expressed in today's lection, namely, the coming of a prophet like Moses. The prophet noted in the text—"like me from among you, from your brethren"—was probably initially intended to refer to the line of prophets which appeared throughout the subsequent history of Israel and Judah. Thus it referred more to the office of prophet and the succession to that office than to a particular prophet per se.

The prophetic task described in this text is multifold: (1) the prophet stands between God and the people just as Moses stood between the assembly and God at the giving of the law at Horeb (probably another name for Mt. Sinai); the prophet is thus one "who stands between"; (2) the prophet is the one to whom the divine will is revealed, the one in whose mouth God's words are put; and (3) the prophet is also the proclaimer of the Word of God to the people. The faithful prophet like Moses is thus the mediator between God and humankind, the recipient of divine revelation, and the proclaimer of that which has been revealed. As such a figure, the prophet can speak and act with divine authorization and authority. Verse 19 declares that when the prophet proclaims what God has revealed then the prophet has fulfilled the major prophetic task. Once this proclamation has taken place, it becomes a matter between God and whomever would not heed the divine words. The text, finally, has Moses warn about the false prophet: whoever speaks a word not commanded by God or whoever speaks in the name of other gods. The false prophet, as elsewhere in Deuteronomy (see 13:1-5), is placed under the penalty of death.

In its original implication, the text on the prophet like unto Moses probably was intended to point to the succession of prophetic spokespersons who appeared throughout Israelite history. Deuteronomy 34:10-12, however, argues that as a prophet no one was Moses' equal, neither in terms of the relationship between God and the prophet nor in terms of the great signs and wonders that he performed. Perhaps Deuteronomy 34:10-12 represents a later interpretation of Moses' prophetic role than Deuteronomy 18:15-20.

At any rate, the text about a prophet like unto Moses came to be understood as the prediction of a single coming prophetic figure, who would appear before the end of time, or the coming of the Messiah. The Qumran community, which produced the Dead Sea Scrolls, for example, expected the figure mentioned in Deuteronomy 18:15-20 to be a herald of the coming eschatological kingdom of God.

The features associated with Moses throughout the Old Testament present a broad picture of his activities—much broader in fact than that of any normal prophet. Moses is pictured as the redemptive leader from Egyptian bondage, as a miracle worker, as a person of authority, as a lawgiver, and as the founder of Israelite religion. Thus to be a prophet like Moses involved an expanded number of roles and functions.

In the Gospel lesson for today, one sees Jesus not only acting as the spokesman who teaches with authority but also as one who carries out redemptive activity, that is, as a prophet like Moses of old.

Psalm 111

This psalm has already been considered as the lesson from the Psalter for the First Sunday After Christmas (see pages 80-81). The reappearance of this psalm here is based on its emphasis on the wonderful works performed by God in the past which can be seen reduplicated in the works of Jesus. The response of the psalmist in verse 10 can, of course, be correlated to the Gospel lesson in that both stress proper and correct understanding.

I Corinthians 8:1-13

The issues discussed in this single chapter are basically similar to those raised in Paul's earlier discussion in I Corinthians 6:12-20, treated earlier in the epistolary reading for the Second Sunday After Epiphany. The immediate topic for discussion is "food offered to idols" (8:1), another question about which the Corinthians had written him. His response actually encompasses chapters 8, 9, and 10, and our text for today is the first part of that response. He returns to these issues specifically in 10:23-30.

Again, one group within the Corinthian church, best understood as an intellectualist minority, was pushing Paul's view of "freedom in Christ" too far (cf. verse 9). Because of their insistence that they could conduct themselves in a radically individualistic fashion, the morale of the whole church was being affected adversely. Paul's ultimate concern is to see that the corporate strength of the church is built up and that the strong become more sensitive to the common good of the whole rather than pushing their individual rights too far.

Paul quotes slogans that were apparently being used and

bandied about within the church: "all of us possess knowledge" (*gnosis*, verse 1); "an idol has no real existence" (verse 4*a*); "there is no God but one" (verse 4*b*). In each of these, "knowledge" (verse 1*b*) is the key word and the underlying attitude giving rise to the problematic position.

With respect to the question of food laws, it is clear that those "in the know" had no particular scruples about food laws. Even if meat bought in a butcher's shop had been previously used in a pagan sacrifice, since their theology was intact (they believed in only one God and knew that idols were not gods but lifeless objects), they could eat it with a clear conscience. And, if they could, why could not every one else who had made the Christian confession in God, the Father, and Christ, the Lord (verse 6).

This was precisely the problem, however. Knowledge does not automatically produce consideration; in fact, quite often it leads the one "in the know" to become impatient with the one "out of the know." The inevitable effect within a group is debilitating with those "in the know" adopting a supercilious stance toward those less gifted and less privileged.

Paul thus opens his remarks by placing knowledge within the demands of love: " 'Knowledge' puffs up, but love builds up" (verse 1*b*). What is more, knowledge is so often self-deceiving and illusory (note, "if any imagines . . ."), and Paul thus reminds his readers that true knowledge consists in recognizing our ignorance. After all, one does not "know God," but is known by God, that is, if there is room at all in the heart for love (verse 3). Paul thus insists that the Corinthians must cease to think of knowledge as the only absolute good. In the church, it must coexist with love.

The latter part of his remarks is directed toward reminding his readers that there are various levels of Christian maturity. The fact is, within every Christian group are those who understand, and perhaps even confess, the Christian creed *theoretically*, but practically they are far from having resolved all the implications this has for them. Pagans recently converted to Christianity required a socialization process through which the ways and means of their new life-style could be constructively assimilated, and this inevitably took time. Paul's advice, essentially, is that Christian knowledge must be tempered by Christian concern for one's brother (and sister). Above all, this will require one to think less of one's own knowledge and individual freedom in Christ and think more of others' lack of knowledge and one's responsibility to behave so that genuine edification of the whole congregation occurs. Adopting such a stance will inevitably mean that the Christian imposes self-restraints, and does so willingly, but Paul saw this as a small price to pay for the sake of a weaker companion in Christ (verse 13).

Mark 1:21-28

Thus far during this Epiphany Season, Jesus has been revealed as King of the Jews, Son of God, Lamb of God, a preacher, and one who calls disciples. In today's Gospel lesson, Jesus is presented as teacher and exorcist. The text does contain a new title, Holy One of God (verse 24), but it is spoken by a demon who is commanded to be silent. A demon speaking the truth is still a demon.

Mark 1:21-28 relates the second of six episodes (1:16-39) by which Mark presents the nature of Jesus' ministry. Although the six events are independent of one another, they have been arranged almost as "a day in the life of Jesus." The text before us is obviously a distinct unit, with verses 21 and 28 providing a typical opening and closing to a story. The account itself, however, is clearly a compound of two stories, one centering on Jesus teaching in the synagogue and the other on an exorcism. Notice verses 21-22 present Jesus as teacher and verse 27 resumes that focus, the crowds being amazed at the authority of his teaching. In between (verses 23-26) is an account of an exorcism, but strikingly that which amazes the crowd is the power of Jesus' teaching. It is not uncommon in Mark to have split stories; that is, one story begins, another episode related but unrelated is told, and then the original story is concluded. Recall, for example, Jesus going to Jairus' house, healing the woman with the blood flow, then continuing on to Jarius' house where he raises the daughter (5:21-34); or the cursing of the fig tree, cleansing the temple, and then finding the fig tree withered

(11:12-26). Obviously verses 21-28 are similarly structured, for reasons we will explore below.

That Jesus was an exorcist all the Gospels except John testify. For Mark it was a centrally important portrayal of Jesus. This was not because exorcizing demons made Jesus unique; other exorcists were at work (Matt. 12:27; Luke 11:19). Nor was Jesus' method of exorcism different from the usual pattern. Accounts of exorcisms usually began with the demon's recognition of the exorcist, the command to come out of the one possessed, the loud and demonstrative departure of the demon, and the amazement of the spectators. That which is most striking in this text is Mark's setting the story of expelling an unclean spirit in the context of Jesus teaching. Quite clearly the exorcism is told to illustrate the power of Jesus' teaching (verse 27).

Given the brevity of Mark, the references to Jesus as teacher are more frequent than in Matthew or Luke. And what is most noticeable is the use of the term in connection with miracles: the teacher stills a storm (4:38), the teacher raises a dead girl (5:35), the teacher feeds the hungry crowd (6:34), the teacher cures an epileptic (9:17), the teacher curses a fig tree (11:21). It is not so much the content of Jesus' teaching that Mark wishes to stress. When Matthew says Jesus taught with authority (7:28-29), the reader is given large blocks of that teaching (chapters 5–7), but in Mark 1:22, essentially the same expression occurs but with no indication of what Jesus said. This is not to say teaching content is totally absent in Mark; chapter 4 is devoted to Jesus' parables. Rather, it is to say that for this Evangelist, the primary emphasis is on the power of Jesus' teaching.

John the Baptist called Jesus "the mightier one" (verse 7), and Jesus himself referred to his mission as entering Satan's house and binding him (3:27). Jesus is the strong Son of God who has entered a world in which the forces of evil (Satan and demons) are crippling, alienating, distorting, and destroying life. According to Mark, the powers that seek to sabotage God's creating and caring work not only cause disease but also disturb the natural elements (4:37-39) and even insinuate themselves into the circle of Jesus' closest friends (8:33). But with Jesus comes the word of power to heal, to help, to give life, and to restore. In Mark, the battle is joined between good and evil, truth and falsehood, life and death, God and Satan. And sometimes, says Mark, the contest is waged in the synagogue! Even the structures of religion may house forces that oppose the gospel.

The preacher will, of course, need to locate and identify the forms and strategies of evil equivalent to the first-century demons. No service is rendered simply by announcing we no longer believe in demons. While that is true for most, not believing in demons has hardly eradicated evil in our world.

Fifth Sunday After Epiphany

Job 7:1-7; Psalm 147:1-11; I Corinthians 9:16-23;
Mark 1:29-39

Even though the time of Epiphany, the time of divine revelation to the world, is not far behind us, the lessons today remind us of another dimension of life and of the Scriptures: divine concealment. Some experiences, even to the faithful, are difficult to understand. Job declares this about his own condition and the psalmist says it about the nameless and forgotten of the earth. Paul engages the Corinthians in a discussion of servitude and freedom that is very difficult to follow, and Mark punctuates his account of Jesus' ministry with one of many statements about the secrecy of Jesus and the confusion of his disciples.

Job 7:1-7

This lesson comprises part of Job's first response (Job 6–7) to the arguments of his "friends" who try to lead him into an understanding of the cause and nature of his misery. It should be recalled from the opening of the book that Job's wealth and health were taken from him as part of a test agreed upon by Satan and God. Job, of course, was unaware of the real factors behind his conditions and thus throughout most of the poetic sections of the book (chapters 3:1–42:6), he maintains his righteousness and argues that he does not deserve his suffering. In the end of the book, Job comes to realize that the divine-human relationship involves more than the question of human righteousness.

The Gospel lesson for today focuses on the healing ministry of Jesus. The passage selected from Job is not concerned with healing or helping but with consideration of some aspects of the human condition that require help and

144

healing. The description of human misery in Job 7:1-7 even leads the author to allow Job to speculate on the advantages of death over against the troubles of human existence (see verses 11-16).

In today's lesson, the author describes some of the qualities of existence viewed through the lenses of human suffering, stressing both the physical and psychological dimensions. First of all, human existence is primarily a life of hard service from which one has only momentary and temporary relief (verses 1-2). Job's days are described as those of a slave or a hireling; there is very little to look forward to. The slave, who gets no pay, can only seek a little comfort by finding a shadow in which to escape the heat of the day. The hireling, the day laborer, can look forward to securing wages but nothing much beyond because they are soon gone or else already spent. Thus life is hard and painful existence with few reliefs of any lasting nature. This type of pessimism about the nature of human existence led some ancient mythologies, for example in the Mesopotamian creation story, to argue that humans were created to be the servants of the gods, created to carry out the tedious chores and back-breaking labors on earth. Life, for Job, was slavery.

Second, Job argues that life is one constant story of agony (verses 3-6). "Months of emptiness" and "nights of misery" are the allotments and apportionments that come his way. Nights are long and days are swift (verses 4, 6). The nights intended for rest are filled with tossing and unrest and lack of sleep. The normal and natural course of events are all set askew and one is forced to live an existence contrary to the way matters should be. The night that should be experienced as passing rapidly becomes a short eternity. Sickness racks the body which is clothed with worms and dirt and replete with sores that close and then reopen.

Verse 7 really begins the section which follows (verses 7-16) but has been combined in our lesson with verses 1-6 as sort of a summary statement of human existence. In what follows verse 7, Job toys with the idea that death is better than life and that death allows one to escape from the bonds of slavery and sickness.

Two themes appear in verse 7. Life is a fleeting, transient, unstable thing, that is, it is a breath without much substance and, like exhaling, is quickly over leaving no permanent record or permanent residue. Second, life is so bleak that Job never expects to see any good again. What the moments given by the breath of life hold open is only a vision of bad not good.

Psalm 147:1-11

This psalm is a hymn of praise about Yahweh and the great acts of the Divine. In many ways, the psalm's intention is to declare that God not only is concerned with and acts in great and universal ways but also that the fate of the weak and insignificant are of ultimate concern as well. The one who is ruler of the world is also the one who is redeemer of the weak. The one who puts the stars in their places and gives them their names is the one who stoops to care for the "nameless," those known by the conditions that plague them. The divine concern with those issues that transcend or overshadow human hurts and heartaches is also the Deity who is immanent to those in need.

The Lord who builds up Jerusalem and returns the exiles, and thus cares for and insures the national life of the people, is also the one who heals the brokenhearted and binds up their wounds (verses 2-3). The one numbering and naming and thus controlling the stars of the heavens is also the one who lifts the downtrodden and topples the wicked to the ground (verses 4-6). The point this psalm is stressing is the mutuality that exists between God's power and God's concern. There is no clash between God's control of the universe and the divine compassion for the weak and the underprivileged.

The downtrodden and the brokenhearted in this psalm probably do not refer to people who were at the bottom of the economic and social totem pole in ancient Israel. There was nothing wrong with such a position in Israel's stratified social structure since most people probably were content, during most periods, to retain the status that birth imposed on them. The downtrodden, brokenhearted, and others were probably those who had suffered some sudden calamity or catastrophe which upset the equilibrium of their lives. Thus the assurance that Yahweh aids these groups is an assurance of concern for those struck by disaster.

The same polarity of divine concern is illustrated in the fact that the same God who controls the weather and rain and makes vegetation grow—the big things in the agricultural year—is also the one who cares for the beasts and the young ravens (verses 8-9).

Two things are most significant for the Deity and evoke the greatest divine pleasure—fear of the Divine (that is, obeying the will of the Deity) and hope in the Deity's steadfast love (verse 11). Fear and hope elicit more pleasure than the strength of horses or men (verse 10).

To stress fear and hope, like seeing the law as the greatest gift to Israel (verses 12-20), is to stress characteristics that one might otherwise think insignificant. How important are the fear and hope of individuals over against the God whose very word of command regulates the universal order? The psalmist does not make explicit why Yahweh finds such pleasure in these qualities though one might conclude that their intrinsic value lies in the fact that they are human responses that cannot be the product of divine coercion or the consequence of divine action in the world of nature.

The assurance that God aids the powerless and cares for those caught in the web of calamity and takes pleasure in those who fear and hope means that life and its worthwhile-ness are not postulated on possessing power, or strength, or wealth but on inner disposition.

I Corinthians 9:16-23

There is a sense in which Paul states in these verses the fundamental principle underlying the various instructions he gives throughout chapters 8–10. This should be stressed since chapter 9 is often regarded as a digression within this larger discussion. It should rather be seen as fully integral to this discussion. Also worth noticing is the fact that all of chapter 9 is couched in an autobiographical mode. The first person is prominent throughout, and it becomes clear that Paul is adducing his own apostolic conduct as exemplary for the Corinthian church to follow. If there is any doubt that he is offering himself as a paradigm for their behavior, this is removed by looking at 10:31–11:1, the concluding section of the entire discussion with the final reminder "Be imitators of me, as I am of Christ."

Immediately being discussed is his own view of his apostolic charge to preach the gospel—his apostleship, in other words (cf. verses 1-2). Through an elaborate set of arguments in verses 3-14, he shows that by all rights and privileges he was entitled to certain inalienable rights as an apostle, chief among these being the right to receive pay for his services. As incontestable as this right was, he had relinquished it for a higher principle: "we have not made use of this right" (to receive pay) to keep from putting an "obstacle in the way of the gospel of Christ" (verse 12).

More important than the particulars of his financial situation—how he supported himself and why—is the underlying motivation for his action. This he spells out in verses 19-23, which are the heart of the pericope.

His remarks are introduced with the freedom/slavery paradox so central to his thought: Christian freedom actually means becoming a slave. He then sketches what appear to be four different groups with whom he was involved during his apostolic ministry: the Jews, probably non-Christian Jews; those under the law, probably Christian Jews; those outside the law, probably non-Christian Gentiles; and the weak, probably Gentile Christians. By being willing to relinquish his human freedom, he had been able to accommodate to these various groups in order to relate the gospel to them. To the final group, however, he had especially accommodated himself. (Note that to each of the first three groups he became "as" each one of them; to the final group he actually became weak.)

But we must ask what fundamental point he is making in these remarks. Is it that he is versatile and accommodating, able to adjust his ministerial life-style to fit any set of circumstances? Or, is it that relating to each group, because of its different demands and viewpoints, has inevitably cost him some of his freedom? It appears to be the latter. To be sure, such willingness to impose limits on his own freedom has caused him to be flexible, but this seems to be the secondary not the primary point.

This line of interpretation is further reinforced by the following paragraph where he introduces the illustration of the athlete in training. The whole point here is that in order to achieve one's ends, one engages in self-discipline, quite often rigorous, and this inevitably entails "self-control" (verse 25).

It is Paul's own willingness to impose limits on his own freedom, to relinquish his own inalienable rights, to deny his own needs, that is in view here. Or, as he summarizes in 10:33, he conducts his apostolic ministry "not seeking my own advantage, but that of many, that they may be saved."

Paul's hope is that the Christian community at Corinth will find his conduct exemplary and will seek to translate his own personal ethic into a congregational life-style. To do so would inevitably mean that the strong would be willing to bear the burdens of the weak, that those "in the know" would be more tolerant of those not "in the know," and that those more practiced and experienced in religious matters would be more patient with those whose conversion to Christianity is their first real exposure to the regimen and ritual of a religion with high ethical demands.

Mark 1:29-39

The Gospel lessons for Epiphany have been thus far quite open and clear in their announcements of who Jesus was and what he was doing. After all, that is what Epiphany means: manifestation or revelation. And next week, on Transfiguration Sunday, the text (Mark 9:2-9) will most vividly declare the glory of God's Son. But today's text, Mark 1:29-39, introduces what seems to be a counter-theme: concealment. Actually the idea of secrecy or silence about Jesus appeared in the Gospel lesson last week in Jesus' rebuke of a demon identifying Jesus as the Holy One of God. "Be silent," Jesus ordered, and expelled the spirit (verse 25). Now that insistence on concealment grows into a larger factor in the narrative, it produces curiosity and confusion in Jesus' followers, then and now. Jesus' call for secrecy and the disciples' inability to understand are two of the most striking characteristics of this Gospel.

The preacher may be inclined not to treat the Gospel reading in the sermon today for reasons quite apart from any internal difficulties. In the first place, the fact that Mark 1:29-39 is not a single unit creates homiletical problems. The text consists of four small units containing enough references to different times and places to indicate that Mark has joined four episodes with very little editorial cement. The first story is the healing of Simon's mother-in-law (verse 29-31); the second concerns healings and exorcisms at sundown (verses 32-34); the third deals with Jesus praying alone in the early morning (verses 35-38); and the last is a summary comment about a Galilee-wide itinerary, preaching and expelling demons (verse 39). In the second place, these stories, while different from previous ones (verses 14-28), actually reveal little that is new about Jesus' identity and ministry. However, after careful reading one finds in this text Mark's introduction of the two themes mentioned in the opening paragraph above. Since those themes will continue throughout this Gospel, no preacher can spend these many weeks in Mark and avoid them.

As Mark has arranged the episodes in our text, they move in this fashion: Jesus becomes extremely popular with the Galileans, Jesus responds to that popularity, and the disciples respond to Jesus. Time and time again Mark calls attention to the growing fame of Jesus: "at once his fame spread everywhere throughout all the surrounding region of Galilee" (verse 28); "the whole city was gathered together about the door" (verse 33); "every one is searching for you" (verse 37); "Jesus could no longer openly enter a town, but was out in the country; and people came to him from every quarter" (verse 45). Some once-popular "Life of Jesus" books called this period "Galilean Spring" in contrast to the later "Jerusalem Winter."

How did Jesus respond to this fame? How was he able to continue to minister to as many as possible and yet not be seduced by popularity? Mark gives four clues. First, according to Mark's arrangement of the stories, scenes of ministry to crowds are followed by scenes of Jesus in private.

Notice: verses 21-28, public; verses 29-31, private; verses 32-34, public; verses 35-38, private; verses 39-45, public; 2:1, private. This public-private pattern may say something not only about Jesus' willingness to serve but also about his need for physical and spiritual recovery. Second, Jesus spends time alone in prayer (verse 35). His disciples see no reason to interrupt a popular tour with retreat and prayer, but to that matter we will return shortly. Third, Jesus moves on to minister to those who have not heard rather than to return to the applause of former ministries (verse 38). And fourth, Jesus sought to silence those who would publicize his name and deeds. This call for silence was given to demons (1:25, 34; 3:12), to those whom he healed (1:44; 5:43; 7:36; 8:26), and to his disciples (8:30; 9:9). To say Jesus was using "reverse psychology," knowing that a prohibition to speak would produce the opposite result, is a woefully inadequate explanation of Mark's portrayal of Jesus. Those who have traveled on the way with Jesus to Golgotha and the empty tomb know that for Mark, the confession of faith in Jesus that is complete and acceptable is at the cross (15:39). The confession of only one who takes up the cross to follow Jesus means more than the compliments of one thousand pushing and shoving in Galilee.

But the disciples do not understand. The first clue to their lack of understanding which will eventually lead to such confusion and fear as to cause them to abandon Jesus (14:50) is given in 1:35-38. Jesus was at prayer in a lonely place. Simon and others pursued (literally, "chased him down"), found him, and interrupted with what they thought was good news—we have a big crowd waiting. In Mark, "searching" for Jesus usually refers to the efforts of those who would distract (3:32; 8:11) or oppose (11:18; 12:12; 14:1, 11, 55). The disciples were correct; there was a crowd, and that is all they saw or wanted to see. They did not understand that there are seekers and there are seekers.

Sixth Sunday After Epiphany (Proper 1)

II Kings 5:1-14; Psalm 32; I Corinthians 9:24-27; Mark 1:40-45

The Gospel lection for today is Mark's account of Jesus healing a leper. Understandably, this story has attracted the account in Second Kings of the healing of Naaman, a leper. Psalm 32 joins one's physical condition to the presence of sin in one's life, sin that must be confessed and forgiven if the body and spirit are to experience refreshing. Paul's autobiographical statement in I Corinthians 9 is a bit distant from the other readings but joins them in referring to one's physical condition as an integral part of one's spiritual well-being.

II Kings 5:1-14

This well-known story of Elisha and Naaman provides an Old Testament narrative parallel to the Gospel reading. Before examining the Naaman story more closely, two general factors should be noted.

First of all, the Elisha cycle of stories (II Kings 2:1–8:6) and thus the career of this prophet seem to belong better with the events in Israelite history associated with King Jehu and his successors rather than with King Ahab. Presently, the stories are placed before Jehu becomes king. If we move these stories from the period of Ahab to the time of the rule of Jehu, then II Kings 2:1–8:6 would fit into the context of II Kings 10:32 and following and Elijah would be the prophet in the stories of II Kings 8:7-15 and 9:1-10. There are several reasons for shifting these stories. Among the more important are the following: (1) the reign of Ahab was one when Israel was strong whereas during Elisha's times, Israel was very weak (as the country was under Jehu and his son Jehoahaz); (2) the prophets were not cooperative with the Israelite monarch while Ahab was king yet Elisha is shown in close cooperation with the Israelite king (see II Kings 3 and 8:1-6); and (3) Israelite-Syrian relations reflected in the Elisha stories are best understood against the historical background of about 843 B.C. following or, that is, after Jehu became king.

Second, the Hebrew term that denotes the illness of Naaman has been translated as "leprosy" but does not refer to the disease today called leprosy. Leprosy (or Hansen's disease) was apparently not present in Palestine in Old Testament times and probably not in New Testament times either. The Hebrew term for the illness (*sarath*) referred to a broad range of skin and fungus infections but not Hansen's disease. That *sarath*, which is discussed in Leviticus 13–14, does not indicate leprosy is indicated by several factors.

1. Descriptions of *sarath* indicate that the sufferer was expected to recover. Leviticus 14 contains directions for purification of the healed sufferer. Hansen's disease or leprosy has of course been incurable.

2. Even clothes and houses could have *sarath* (see Lev. 13:47-59) or some type of fungus or mildew infection.

3. Human skeletons unearthed in archaeological excavations in Palestine do not indicate the presence of Hansen's disease. Hansen's disease was called elephantiasis in ancient times. In the Middle Ages, *lepra* the Greek term used to translate *sarath* also came to be used for elephantiasis and this produced the confusion.

The story of Naaman's healing develops through the course of several scenes.

1. After verse 1 sets the stage by identifying the central character, the scene shifts to the Israelite maiden (verses 2-3). The Israelite girl, a captive subjected to menial house duties in a foreign land, stands as a contrast to Naaman, the powerful general.

2. In scene two (verses 4-5), the Syrian administration turns the proposed journey to Samaria (note that Elisha is "the" prophet of Samaria in verse 3) into a major production: royal commissioning of the trip, an advance letter to set the stage, and enough gifts to have financed a hospital.

3. In scene three (verses 6-7), the letter arrives for the king of Israel who thinks he is the one to heal Naaman. Of course,

the Israelite king at the time was the weakest of monarchs and no doubt was the butt of many stories. As a vassal to Syria, he was a weakling who could exercise no power. Thus his response to the letter probably was intended to produce laughter when the story was told to Israelite audiences.

4. Again, it is the person at the periphery, this time, Elisha, who is the real representative of power in the story. In this scene (verses 8-12), the Syrian general becomes the humiliated one. Expecting his cure to be a showcase extravaganza, he is treated instead to a visit from a subordinate messenger and the order to dip himself seven times in the Jordan. His response is that there are better rivers in Syria than the muddy old Jordan. The hearer of this story could realize the point: maybe Syria has better rivers than Israel but Israel has something better—namely its God.

5. In this last scene (verses 13-14), it is again the lowly and the peripheral—the servants of the great one—who talk the master into obedience. Seven dunks in the river Jordan and Naaman emerged cleansed.

Psalm 32

This thanksgiving psalm has been chosen to accompany the other readings because a condition within which thanksgiving would be appropriate results in both the Old Testament and Gospel readings. Naaman is healed of his "leprosy" and thus becomes clean and able to participate in all areas of life. Uncleanliness prevented one from participating in certain religious observances and from entry into temple precincts.

Such a psalm as 32 was used within services of thanksgiving in which three basic elements figured. (1) The worshipers offered testimony about both the conditions under which they had suffered and the facts of their redemption by God. (2) A thanksgiving sacrifice was offered in which the Deity received a portion and the worshipers and their families and friends consumed the remainder. The meat of a thanksgiving sacrifice had to be consumed on the day of the sacrifice (see Lev. 7:12-15). This encouraged conspicuous consumption and celebration, as well as sharing. (3) Instruction based on the redeemed's experience was offered to family, friends, and whatever audience was in attendance.

The following is the form-critical structure of the psalm: (a) pronouncements of blessedness spoken about or to the one offered thanksgiving, probably spoken by the priest to the worshiper or to the worshiper and the attending congregation (verses 1-2); (b) the description, in the form of a thanksgiving prayer to the Deity, of the condition from which the worshiper was saved (verses 3-5); (c) a prayer to the Deity formulated as an indirect call to prayer by those in attendance (verse 6); (d) the prayer response (verse 7); and (e) instruction by the one offering thanksgiving to those in attendance at the service (verses 8-11).

The opening pronouncements of happiness or blessedness in verses 1-2 were probably proclaimed by a cultic official or priest (the religious staff person in charge of the service). The two blessings are almost identical in context with only slight variations in certain nuances. In these verses three elements are noted: the sinner, the sin, and the Deity. The opening verse declares sinners happy or blessed when transgression is forgotten (a better translation than RSV's "forgiven") and sin is covered. Forgotten and covered indicate that the acts of the past are truly forgiven and gone.

Verse 2 declares happy the one "whom the Lord does not hold guilty" (NJPSV). That is, happy is the person who through sacrifice and confession has made amends with the Deity. The last half of verse 2 refers to the one "in whose spirit there is no deceit" or, better, the one who shows no hesitancy about rectifying matters of sin and wrongdoing.

In the description of the earlier distress, in verses 3-5, the psalmist coordinates four factors: (a) lack of repentance followed by (b) sickness and strain and (c) confession followed by (d) forgiveness. In ancient Israel, acknowledgment and confession of sin, as well as restitution to injured parties, were essential ingredients in the repentance process. From a therapeutic or psychological point of view, one can say that the psalm writer was fully aware of the need for the sinner to tell his/her story as a form of self-identity and self-enlightenment and thus to claim responsibility for wrongdoing. In II Samuel 12:1-14, Nathan tells the "confessional" story with which David then identifies. In ancient Israelite theology, without confession, there was no forgiveness of sin.

The association of sickness and unconfessed sin, noted in verses 3-4, illustrates the close psychosomatic connection between physical and mental health—a connection that is being recognized more and more in contemporary culture. Although the physical consequences are described as the result of unconfessed sins, they are also spoken of as the result of divine action as well ("thy hand was heavy upon me"). This suggests that the understanding of human sentiments and feelings and the understanding of divine actions are closely interrelated.

Verse 5 contains something of the exuberance that comes after long-seething and secret sin is allowed to surface and be exposed to the light of day. The articulation, the coming to expression, of the nagging problem is the first step toward healing. Note that three expressions are used for this unveiling of the suppressed sin—acknowledged, did not hide, will confess. The close connection between confession and forgiveness is affirmed in the recognition that following confession "then thou didst forgive the guilt of my sin."

This section of the psalm (verses 3-5) can be an ideal text for the minister to use in addressing the issues of human sinfulness, confession, and forgiveness. The sentiments and conditions described in the psalm are certainly appropriate for contemporary people. The latter, however, frequently assumes that what one does with wrongdoing is to "stuff" it or keep it under wraps—the exact sentiments seen to be so destructive in the psalm.

Verses 6-11 are to be seen in the context of the thanksgiving ritual in which the worshiper calls upon those attending the service (friends, family, associates) to join in the celebration and to learn from the experience that the worshiper has gone through. The redeemed pleads with his audience not to be stubborn like some dumb animal. That is, they are not to be like the worshiper was before the acknowledgment and confession of sin (verses 3-4).

I Corinthians 9:24-27

In today's epistolary reading, two athletic images are prominent: the runner and the boxer. They form a fitting conclusion to chapter 9, in which Paul has spoken of his self-restraint as an apostle.

The question of eating sacrificial meats (I Cor. 8:1) had exposed certain flaws in the corporate life of the Corinthian church. The "strong" were secure in their "knowledge" (I Cor. 8:1), but were less practiced in "love" (I Cor. 8:1-3). They were apparently more accustomed to answering to their own yearnings for individual expression than responding to the needs of weaker Christians. Consequently, in his earlier remarks Paul urges a corporate ethic in which members think less of their individual freedom and more of the common good (I Cor. 8:9). To reinforce this form of exhortation, Paul adduces his own apostolic behavior as an example for the Corinthians to follow. Specifically, he was entitled to receive pay for his work as an apostle (I Cor. 9:3-12), but he had chosen consistently to relinquish this right (I Cor. 9:12-18). It was a clear case of giving up an "inalienable right" for the sake of the gospel. His hope was that his own practice in this respect would serve as an example for the Corinthians.

It was typical practice among Greco-Roman moralists to provide both positive and negative examples to reinforce their ethical teachings. Thus, along with his own apostolic behavior as a positive example, he introduces Israel as a negative example (I Cor. 10:1-13). Whereas he exemplified self-restraint, Israel exemplified self-indulgence.

But before discussing Israel, he concludes his discussion of his own apostolic self-restraint with an everyday illustration drawn from the world of athletics (I Cor. 9:24-27). The images of the runner and the boxer are introduced as familiar images: "You know (do you not?) that . . . " (verse 24, NEB). They are especially appropriate given the prominence of the Isthmian games in the vicinity of Corinth. For centuries, Corinthians had witnessed these biennial games that had made runners and boxers, along with orators, dramatists, and poets, familiar figures participating in the festivals.

But one need not have been an inhabitant of Corinth to

grasp the significance of these images. They were well publicized throughout the Empire, both through artistic depictions and popular speech. Not surprisingly, they become common metaphors in the New Testament. Paul pursues the "not yet" of the resurrection faith as a runner "straining forward to what lies ahead . . . [pressing] on toward the goal for the prize" (Phil. 3:13-14; cf. I Tim. 1:18; cf. also Heb. 12:1). "Fighting the good fight" (I Tim. 1:18; 6:12; II Tim. 4:7) recalls the images of the boxer, or wrestler. We are thus urged to "contend [earnestly] for the faith" (Jude 3).

In today's text, Paul is reminding us of the obvious: many compete, but one wins (verse 24). Rather than despairing of the competition, we are urged to "run to win!" (verse 24, NEB). The motivation is not a "fading wreath" (verse 25). This may recall the practice, apparently distinctive at the Isthmian games, of rewarding the winners with a wreath of withered celery, as opposed to the fresh, green wreaths that were used at other games, such as the Olympian games. An unfading wreath, by contrast, awaits the Christian athlete who hopes for the eschatological crown of life (cf. II Tim. 2:5; 4:8; I Pet. 5:4; James 1:12; Rev. 2:10; 3:11).

But the main point of today's text seems to lie elsewhere: the need for "strict training" (verse 25; *egkrateia*). The fundamental notion here is "self-control," the capacity to impose limits on oneself for the sake of a higher, nobler good. It is an attribute that is counted among the Christian virtues (Gal. 5:23; II Pet. 1:6), a worthy topic of preaching deemed attractive to pagans (Acts 24:25), and sufficiently important to be a qualification for an elder in the church (Titus 1:8). This point is elaborated toward the end of our passage as Paul insists that he is no shadow boxer. Rather, he bruises his own body, making it know its master (verse 27, NEB). The athlete willingly inflicts pain for the sake of self-discipline, knowing that a life without any restraints will lead to softness and in the end to rejection.

The effect of this set of athletic images is to call us to a life of discipline in which we impose restraints on our behavior for the sake of a higher good. In this case, the higher good is the good of the congregation, the people of God. What is needed is the capacity to relinquish certain "freedoms," which by all rights are ours, but which may not necessarily be edifying to the whole church.

Mark 1:40-45

Mark's story of Jesus healing a leper is shared by both Matthew (8:2-4) and Luke (5:12-16), both of whom have it in briefer form. Luke also has an account of Jesus healing ten lepers (17:11-19). Mark locates the event quite early, the last in a series of six vignettes (1:16-45) in which Mark shows the nature of Jesus' ministry, its location, its power, and its public impact. Jesus is a preacher, a teacher, an exorcist, and a healer. But the reader is not, like the crowds, to be caught in a spell of undifferentiated amazement. Rather the reader is to ask, What is it really that Jesus is doing?

Last Sunday's lection ended with Jesus on a ministry tour of Galilee. Apparently during that tour the healing of the leper occurred. Luke says he was in one of the cities (5:12). Lepers, while they were required to distance themselves (Luke 17:12) from others, crying, "Unclean, unclean!" tended to gather near centers of population in order to collect alms. As outcasts they were not permitted in places of employment. (For the Jewish regulations about leprosy and lepers, cf. Lev. 13–14.) Apparently leprosy designated a number of sin diseases ranging from serious to non-serious. Even clothes and houses contracted leprosy, possibly a kind of mildew or rot. At any rate, for one to show signs of having this disease meant that one was ritually and religiously unclean, not allowed in places of worship. One was also socially ostracized, separated from family, friends, and all public life. The economic effects were, of course, devastating since all business and employment ceased. The leper is a corpse haunting the edges of the community he can no longer enter.

So desperate is this leper that he crosses the distance that he should observe and approaches Jesus (verse 40). Directly or indirectly he has come to the belief that Jesus has the power to heal him. The only barrier—"If you *will*" (verse 40). The preacher may wish to note the difference between "if you will" here and "if you can" at Mark 9:23. Jesus responds quite differently to the two approaches. In the healing, Jesus touched the leper, putting him at risk of having to join the leper colony himself. This is important for understanding Jesus' ministry and that of those who would continue his work. Jesus did not minister long distance, safe from all that plagued the lives of those he would help. His work of forgiving brought him in contact with sinners; his work of lifting placed him among the fallen; his words of encouragement were given among the hopeless; his healing put him with the diseased; his giving new life took him to the tomb.

That Jesus healed the man meant more than a change in skin texture. The domestic, social, religious, and economic effects are immediately evident.

No preacher will want to treat this as an isolated miracle, as a private blessing, as another "Jesus and I" story. The fabric of healthy relationships is mended. Jesus has struck a blow at one of the forces that cripples, alienates, and destroys human life. To reduce the ministry of Jesus and the ministry of the church to some inner change in the soul is just that, a reduction.

Following the healing, the leper is given two instructions. First, be quiet about what happened. This is not a case of Jesus using reverse psychology in an effort to advertise his ministry. Jesus wants no publicity; he wishes people to come to faith understanding who he is and what he is about. He is not seeking to be a star, known for relieving people of burdens and difficulties. All the way to the cross Jesus will be trying to get those who think "where the Messiah is, there is no misery" to accept a new perspective—"where there is misery, there is the Messiah."

The second instruction: Follow the requirements of the law and go through the ritual of restoration with the priest (verse 44; Lev. 14:2-32). Disregarding law and tradition does not in itself prove that one is a new person.

That the healed man could not contain the news of his restoration should not be viewed harshly. In retrospect, one wonders if the Christian cause might not be better served if only those who had something significant to report were allowed to speak, all others keeping quiet. But it must be said that the man's broadcasting had a negative effect on Jesus' ministry (verse 45). The publicity created audiences not congregations, and Jesus had to avoid the towns, keeping himself in the countryside. But still they came to him from everywhere, and understandably so.

Seventh Sunday After Epiphany (Proper 2)

Isaiah 43:18-25; Psalm 41; II Corinthians 1:18-22; Mark 2:1-12

The texts for today affirm the gracious activity of God toward us in spite of our sin and weakness. This is especially affirmed, says Paul in II Corinthians 1, in Jesus Christ who is God's yes to us. God says yes to a forgetful and stubborn people, says Isaiah, again forgiving their transgressions. Psalm 41 testifies to a healing, forgiving, and vindicating visit from the Lord, and Mark, in an unusual story, tells of Jesus granting forgiveness and healing in the life of a man who needed both.

Isaiah 43:18-25

That Isaiah 40–55 stems from an anonymous prophet who preached to Jewish exiles in Babylon just before the capture of the city by Cyrus is now almost universally conceded. Deutero- or Second Isaiah, as this unknown speaker is designated, had several goals in mind: (1) to convince the exiles that their stay in Babylon as punishment was sufficient penalty for their sins was one objective (see Isa. 40:1-2); (2) Deutero-Isaiah wanted to convince the exiles that God was still in control of history and that the budding conquest of the Persians was the work of Yahweh (see Isa. 45:1-7); and (3) the divinely guided events of history were soon to result in the release of the exiles and their return to the homeland. It is the last of these objectives that is the focus of today's lection.

All of 43:18-25 is presented as a divine speech addressed to the exiles. It is difficult to know where the unit of which verses 18-25 is a part really begins and ends. It at least includes verses 16 through 28.

Verses 18-19a form the linchpin in the speech: "remember

not the former things, nor consider the things of old. Behold, I am doing a new thing." Interpreters have long discussed what the expression "former things" refers to. (1) Is this a reference back to the great salvation events of Israel's past—the Exodus from Egypt? The imagery in verses 19*b*-21 might suggest this. (2) Or are the former things those events immediately preceding the destruction of Jerusalem and the beginning of the Exile? Verses 27-28 would suggest this since verse 27 talks about the "former father who sinned" (probably an allusion to King Zedekiah) whose rebellion brought an end to the sanctuary (the destruction of the temple in 586 B.C.).

If the reference is to (1) then Deutero-Isaiah is telling the exilic audience that the great events of the Exodus can be forgotten since something greater is on its way. One could doubt, however, if anyone in ancient Israel would have advised an audience to forget the Exodus, the central feature in Israel's symbolic world! If the reference is to the events associated with the beginning of the Exile, then Deutero-Isaiah is telling the hearers that they can forget the preaching of judgment that preceded the fall of Jerusalem. The words of judgment are over; God is now ready to do a new and totally different thing. The day of salvation is at hand.

The forthcoming salvation will be analogous to the Exodus: God will make a way through the wilderness between Babylonia and Palestine (verse 19*b*) just as he made a way through the sea when the Hebrews came out of Egypt (verse 16; see Isa. 11:16; Exod. 14). The inhospitable desert will be transformed and the wilderness wildlife will acknowledge and honor Yahweh (see Isa. 11:6-9). The function of the redeemed community is to praise Yahweh (verse 21*b*). Redemptive and redeemed existence is here presented as celebration.

Verses 22-24 appear to be highly condemnatory of the people. They are formulated in such a way as to highlight verse 25. Verses 22-24 declare that there is nothing in the people's actions and behavior that constitutes the basis and grounds for divine redemption. Instead it is Yahweh who of his own free will and for his own sake wipes away the people's transgressions and remembers their sins no more. The gospel was the gospel even in the Old Testament!

Psalm 41

This psalm concludes the first book of the Psalter. This is indicated by the doxology found in verse 13. (Most modern translations such as the RSV, actually insert a heading "Book II" following verse 13 although no such statement is found in the Hebrew text.) Other such doxologies are found in Psalms 72:18-20; 89:52; and 106:48. These doxologies divide the book of Psalms into five books. These five books were probably constituted to be read in conjunction with the five books of the Torah (Pentateuch). A consecutive portion of the Torah and a psalm would have been read weekly in synagogue services so that Genesis would have been read along with the first book of Psalms (Pss. 1–41), Exodus with book two (Pss. 42–72), and so on. In a three-year lectionary, all of the Pentateuch and all of the Psalms would have been read and the process begun again.

Psalm 41 is the prayer of one ailing, living surrounded by enemies, and awaiting healing and the opportunity to get back at the enemies. In a fashion, the plight of the worshiper in this psalm is analogous to that of the ill person in the Gospel lesson although in the psalm even the person's closest associate offered no consolation but only further ridicule.

Verses 1-3 of the psalm appear to have been spoken by the priest or a cultic/worship leader in charge of the service of personal intercession. The content of these verses is primarily addressed to a human audience but is not confessional in nature (note that God is addressed in verses 2b and 3b). The opening verses seem to promise that God will show mercy and concern for those who show mercy and concern: "Happy is he who is thoughtful of the wretched; / in bad times may the Lord keep him from harm" (verse 1, NJPSV).

The supplication of the sick person begins in verse 4. In the opening plea, the request for grace and healing is connected with sin. It is not said that sin is the cause of the sickness; the two are simply connected as in the Gospel reading.

In one of the Dead Sea Scrolls (the so-called Nabonidus text), a story is told of how the Babylonian king was healed by a Jewish exorcist after his sins had been announced forgiven.

The sickness may not have been considered so much the consequence or result of the sin as a warning to alert the person of something wrong in his life. The author of Ecclesiasticus (or Sirach) warned those who were sick to "give up your faults and direct your hands aright, / and cleanse your heart from all sin" (38:10).

The psalm is as much concerned with the ill person's human relations as with the sickness. Enemies already anticipate the sufferer's death (verse 5). Visitors spread rumors about the victim's condition (verse 6). Others whisper about the person's condition, always imagining the worst (verse 7). People make their own prognosis of the disease (verse 8) and even close companions can no longer be relied upon (verse 9).

We might pause to ask why ancient clerics who wrote the Psalms would have worshipers express their feelings and conditions in this form. (1) First of all, when persons become ill, particularly terminally ill, the world does or at least may appear to take a different attitude toward them. (2) Isolation from social life and withdrawal from the routines of life create a strong sense of alienation. The psalm writers probably felt that it was best to verbalize such feelings even if the sick had to be compelled to speak them rather than let the feelings exist unarticulated. (3) Even the feeling that sin and sickness are somehow related is better expressed than merely left to brew. The natural human reaction to calamity is to ask, What did I do to deserve this? (4) The statements about friends, enemies, and other associates force the sick person to focus on the divine–human relationship. People have to realize that when the worst comes there is nothing much others can do. The road to the cemetery is ultimately traveled alone. (Except in war, few people died very quickly in antiquity.)

The psalm closes with an upbeat attitude (verses 10-12). At least God can be counted on.

But, You, O Lord, have mercy on me;
> let me rise again and repay them.
Then shall I know that You are pleased with me:
> when my enemy cannot shout in triumph over me.
You will support me because of my integrity,
> and let me abide in Your presence forever. (NJPSV)

II Corinthians 1:18-22

Of the many ways Christ is presented in the New Testament, today's epistolary passage is one of the most distinctive and unusual: Christ as God's yes. One of the things that makes this christological claim so striking is that it is not a personal metaphor, as is so often the case: Christ as Son of God, Son of man, high priest, Savior. Rather, the christological "title" in this case is an adverb!

What prompts this highly unusual way of speaking of Christ is a controversy involving Paul's own behavior. From the preceding verse, it becomes clear that some of Paul's opponents accused him of being "vacillating" and acting like a "worldly man" (verse 17). Elsewhere, it appears that some objected to the two faces Paul presented: strong in print, weak in person (II Cor. 10:10). What emerges is a perception of Paul as someone who is unreliable, who cannot be counted on to do what he promises, who makes plans and changes them, who says both yes and no, who speaks out of both sides of his mouth.

Naturally, these charges raise Paul's ire, so he speaks in his own defense. First, he grounds his defense in the character of God: "As surely as God is faithful" (verse 18). That God is faithful becomes something of an axiom in the New Testament, perhaps because of its strong Old Testament underpinnings (Deut. 7:9; Ps. 145:13). It can be a word of reassurance used to conclude a prayer (I Cor. 1:9) or to reinforce a word of exhortation (I Cor. 10:13; II Thess. 3:3). It is often used in an eschatological context to reassure us that God is capable of delivering us to our ultimate destiny (I Thess. 5:24; also I Cor. 1:9). The fidelity of God is unaffected by the infidelity of humans: even "if we are faithless, [God] remains faithful" (II Tim. 2:13). God's faithfulness can be linked with God's promises: what God promises, God delivers (Heb. 10:23; 11:11). Especially is this true of the promise of forgiveness (I John 1:9).

The reason that Paul can so closely identify his own behavior with the faithfulness of God is that it is finally "God who establishes us . . . in Christ, has commissioned us . . . [and] has put his seal upon us and given us his Spirit in our hearts" (verses 21-22). As one commissioned by God, Paul sees himself as God's co-worker (II Cor. 6:1), as the one through whom God appeals to humanity (II Cor. 5:20). The assumption here is that Paul's message is an extension of God's voice: "in the sight of God we speak in Christ" (II Cor. 2:17).

Given this close identification between God's message and Paul's voice, he can claim that his word and conduct are unambiguous: "the language in which we address you is not an ambiguous blend of Yes and No" (verse 18, NEB). And why? Because Jesus Christ is "the Yes pronounced upon God's promises, every one of them" (verse 20, NEB). Paul could insist that Jesus Christ was the essence of what he preached (II Cor. 4:5). But more than this, Paul insisted that Christ was the one in whom God confirmed "the promises given to the patriarchs" (Rom. 15:8). All the promises that littered the history of God's people from the time of Abraham forward finally found their yes in Christ, the "end of the law" (Rom. 10:4; Gal. 3:29).

Because God has said yes to us through Christ, when we pray and "give glory to God" (verse 20, NEB), we say "amen" to God through Christ. Our yes in prayer meets God's yes in Christ. God's unambiguous affirmation is met by our unambiguous prayer offered in faith. It is in keeping with this train of thought that the Johannine Apocalypse speaks of Christ himself as "the Amen" (Rev. 3:14).

God has done more than spoken. God has also acted and acted decisively in confirming the yes of the divine promises. By giving the Spirit within our hearts "as a guarantee" (verse 22; cf. 5:5; Rom. 8:23; Eph. 1:14), God has imprinted us with the divine seal that marks us decisively as belonging to Christ (cf. Eph. 1:13). In this way, the yes of God's Word, mediated through the preached Christ, becomes engraved in our hearts, and our lives become as unambiguous yesses in God's behalf as God has become in ours.

The homiletical possibilities of this text are many. For one thing, the preacher might consider the ways in which God has said yes to humanity through Christ. The many contexts in which yes is uttered, and the decisive difference it can make, provide numerous ways for us to reflect on Christ as God's yes. Our text suggests that through the sending of Christ, God finally tilted in our favor with an emphatic declaration in our behalf. We should not conclude that it was a begrudging yes, a qualified yes, a muffled yes. "With him it was, and is, Yes" (verse 19, NEB). Period.

Mark 2:1-12

Having given a dramatically brief sketch of Jesus' ministry and his sudden rise to great popularity in Galilee, Mark now presents the darker side of that ministry: conflict and controversy. In 2:1–3:6 Mark records five of these clashes, stating the issue, the opponents, and Jesus' way of dealing with it. Very likely the early church preserved these stories to provide guidance for its own handling of criticism and debate. Our lesson today, 2:1-12 (also in Matt. 9:1-8; Luke 5:17-26), is the first of these controversies.

The event occurred in Capernaum where Jesus was "at home" or "in a house" (2:1). Mark frequently remarks that some act or teaching of Jesus took place "in a house" (7:17, 24; 9:28, 33; 10:10). This expression not only serves Mark's overall emphasis on Jesus' desire for privacy and resistance to instant success but also enables Mark to distinguish between private and public teaching. Sometimes Jesus is in a house; sometimes he is pressed by the crowds. In 2:1, his being pressed by the crowds while in a house is a union of the two scenes into one, setting the stage for high drama.

The preacher will notice immediately some unusual features of this story. In it are joined two ministries of Jesus, healing the sick and forgiving sin, and the two are joined by the repetition of the phrase, "he said to the paralytic" (verses 5, 10). In fact, the issue of forgiveness occupies the central verses (6-10) and healing is the subject matter in verses 3-5,

11-12. More awkward is the joining of the two ministries in terms of which is easier and which is harder (verse 9). The category of relative difficulty hardly seems to fit. In addition, in verses 10-11, healing the cripple is offered as proof of authority to forgive sins. Neither in Judaism or Christianity did power to heal imply or infer power to forgive sins. Only God can forgive (verse 7). Forgiving sin was never associated with the work of the expected Messiah. For Jesus, and by implication, for the church to announce forgiveness of sins was an act of a person or persons representing God and speaking God's word of grace. The discontinuity between the healing and the forgiving is also evident in the conclusion to the story. That which amazed the crowd was the healing not the forgiving (verse 12), even though the forgiveness of sins was far more remarkable. Could it be the crowd was aware only of the healing? And Mark says *all* were "amazed and glorified God" (verse 12). Does that include the questioning and accusing scribes of verses 6-7?

These features of Mark 1:1-12 have led many students of the passage to theorize that Mark has joined two stories by inserting into a healing (verses 1-5, 11-12) an account of Jesus' forgiving sin (verses 6-10). Inserting one story into another is a familiar literary pattern in this Gospel. Recall, for example, the account of raising Jairus' daughter (5:21-24, 35-43) into which Mark places the healing of the woman with the blood flow (verses 25-34). Mark 11:12-25 is another example. This theory relieves the passage of many of its literary and logical difficulties.

However, whether it is treated as a unit describing a single event or a Markan construction joining two events, 2:1-12 offers to the preacher and the listeners several strong themes. The passage announces clearly the power of Jesus over sin and disease. That sin and suffering are joined in the human condition is the testimony of both Scripture (Gen. 3; John 5:14; 9:2; Rom. 8:18-26) and experience. This is not to say that the Scriptures subscribe to modern psychosomatic views or that every case of suffering signals the presence of a sinful act. Jesus shattered the notion that anyone suffering is guilty of some sin both by his word (John 9:3) and in his own crucifixion. Jesus did not suffer because he had sinned, but because others did. Rather the Bible joins sin and suffering in a more cosmic sense, alienation from God being the root cause of all human woes. As a minor theme, the preacher may wish to comment on the representation of faith in the story. It is not that of the paralytic but of those who brought him (verse 5). Here is the church in miniature: a person being sustained by the faith of others when one's own condition, physical, spiritual, or mental, is, at least temporarily, far short of sufficient.

Eighth Sunday After Epiphany (Proper 3)

Hosea 2:14-20; Psalm 103:1-13; II Corinthians 3:1-6; Mark 2:18-22

If the preacher would find a theme common to the lessons for today surely it would be the affirmation that God is continually doing a new thing, creating anew and entering into new covenants. God's new activity cannot be confined in the old wineskins or clothed by repairing the old garment (Mark 2). Both Paul (II Cor. 3) and Hosea refer to God as the maker of new covenants. God has done wondrous things in the past, says the psalmist, but those are not to be recited as the sum of what God does. In fact, the past pales before the new creative and redeeming activity of God toward us.

Hosea 2:14-20

Running through all texts for this Sunday is the theme of newness, of a new covenant, or of a new relationship to God. For Hosea, the image is that of a new relationship with Yahweh at the beginning of their history together.

Hosea had used his wife Gomer to symbolize the relationship between Israel and Yahweh. Thus the relationship was depicted in marriage and sexual terms. Verses 14-20 describe the renewal of the Yahweh-Israel "marriage." Hosea anticipated that judgment was soon to come against Israel, in the form of an Assyrian invasion, which would leave the country in dire straits (see 3:4). Beyond the judgment and the punishment, the prophet spoke of a good time coming, which is depicted in verses 14-20.

Verses 14-15 describe Yahweh's renewed courtship of Israel. The place of the romantic undertaking will be back in the wilderness where Hosea claims Yahweh originally found Israel "like grapes in the wilderness" (9:10). Yahweh will

171

allure Israel for a rendezvous in the desert and there court her again, speaking tenderly to her (literally, "upon the heart"). Like the husband, Yahweh will bestow gifts upon her ("her vineyards") and like a new bridegroom will lead her to a new start in the land. The Valley of Achor ("Trouble") refers to the locale where Israel, in the person of Achan, was disobedient in the account of the initial conquest (see Josh. 7). The old valley of trouble will become the doorway of hope, the path of a new life.

In the wilderness, Israel will be a loyal and responsive bride responding as she did in the original journey from Egypt (verse 15b). Here Hosea draws upon the view that the time Israel initially spent in the wilderness between Egypt and the Promised Land was a good time marked by obedience and good relations. This portrayal is also found in Deuteronomy 8:1-4; 29:5; Jeremiah 2:1-3. (Most of the Old Testament, however, describes the stay in the wilderness as a time of murmuring and disobedience.)

Israel's new relationship to Yahweh will mean that she can address God as "my husband" (literally "my man") and no longer as "my Baal" ("my lord" or "my husband"). Presumably the prophet is here emphasizing that the word "Baal" will no longer be used by the Israelites. This is the clear sense of verse 17 which refers to the removal of the names of the Baals from her mouth. Verse 16 thus implies that the Israelites, in the eyes of the prophet, had been worshiping Yahweh as if he were merely another of the Baals. The god Baal was worshiped throughout the area of Syria-Palestine as the god of the rainy season and the deity of fertility. Baal was a dying-rising god who (as the power of fertility in vegetation and animal life) died in the late spring with the onset of the summer drought. He was resurrected in the fall with the coming of the rainy season and the renewed growth of vegetation. Associated with Baal worship were possible fertility/sexual rites performed in imitation of the actions of the god Baal and his heavenly consort (see 2:13). The reference to Baals is probably due to the fact that Baal worship differed slightly from place to place. One would have worshiped the Baal of Shechem, the Baal of Tyre, and so on with slightly different rituals.

As part of the new arrangement, Yahweh promises to establish several new conditions. First of all, reference is made to Yahweh's establishment of a treaty or covenant between Israel and the various components of the animal kingdom: wild animals (beasts of the field), birds of the air, and creeping things of the ground. This would include all the animal kingdom except for domesticated animals (for the various classes, see Gen. 1:20-25, although water creatures are omitted in Hosea's statement). The prophet apparently conceives of God redoing the orders of creation and bringing the human and animal kingdoms into close harmony and reconciliation (see Isa. 11:6-9). Note here that the covenant is not between Yahweh and the people but between the people and the animals. God is the mediator, not the subject of the covenant relationship.

Second, peace will prevail in the land (verse 18b). The bow and the sword (the military armaments) and warfare itself will be destroyed from the land and people can rest in safety. Like Isaiah 2:4, this text gives expression to the universal longing of a world without war. The land of Palestine, so frequently drenched with the blood of battle, was also washed with tears shed from eyes longingly looking for peace.

Third, Yahweh promises to betroth Israel to himself forever and offers to her righteousness, justice, steadfast love, and mercy as the bridal gifts to the betrothed (verse 19). Possessing these, the future Israel will be faithful. In Israelite life, betrothal was a binding, legal obligation requiring the equivalent of a divorce to break its binding quality. Here God then is committing himself anew to marriage with Israel.

Finally, Israel "shall know the Lord" ("be devoted to the Lord," NJPSV) for she will be betrothed in faithfulness (verse 20). Israel would possess the knowledge of Yahweh that for so long had been lacking in the land (see 4:1).

Psalm 103:1-13

This psalm may be understood as a meditation on theology and anthropology or the divine-human relationship. It is essentially a psalm of thanksgiving but thanksgiving expressed in hymnic form. The psalm contains no direct address to the Deity nor does it describe any predicament from which the worshiper has been redeemed. The text has a homiletical flavor about it.

On the basis of content, the psalm may be seen as expounding on the activity of God (verses 1-6), the nature of the divine-human relationship (verses 7-14), and transitory human life in the embrace of divine mercy and fidelity (verses 15-19).

The composition begins as a self addressing the self (verse 1). In the final stanza, the range of vision is greatly expanded, arching out to include the angels, the heavenly hosts, and all the works of creation.

The verses selected for the lection are fundamentally theological affirmations; their content is composed of descriptive statements about God. If we include verse 6 with verses 1-5, and this is a possible although not an obvious division, then the first six verses speak of seven deeds of the Deity:

A. forgives iniquity
B. heals diseases
C. redeems from the Pit
X. crowns with steadfast love and mercy
C.' satisfies with good as long as one lives
B.' renews youthful vigor like that of an eagle
A.' works vindication and justice for all oppressed

The depiction of these actions—structured in an ABCXC'B'A' scheme—are expressed through participial forms of the verbs. One might take such formulations, like participles in English, as describing states of being. Thus the actions denoted are taken as descriptions characteristic of the Deity.

Verses 8-13 contain a second series, this time comprising six items that describe the character of Yahweh, particularly with regard to the divine reaction to human error, wrongdoing, and rebellion. Verse 14 should be considered in conjunction with these verses since it offers anthropological insight and rationale for divine behavior, offering reasons anchored in human existence for God's grace and mercy.

Throughout this section, descriptions of God's treatment of the sinner and explanations of divine behavior are interlaced. Each verse makes independent but interrelated points.

1. God's nature is oriented to mercy and grace; he is not easily upset and when he is, there is mercy abounding (verse 8).

2. God does not perpetually torment or nag incessantly since his anger does not abide forever. The text does not deny that God has anger and that he does react in wrath; however, the divine is willing to let bygones be bygones (verse 9).

3. God does not operate on a tit-for-tat basis. The punishment is not made to fit the crime. God is free to reduce the penalty, to soften the shock of human actions (verse 10).

4. Divine mercy is compared to the greatness of the heights of the heaven above the earth (verse 11).

5. The vertical dimension used in verse 11 is replaced by a horizontal dimension in describing the removal of trans-gressions. East and west, or literally the rising and setting (of the sun), is a way of stressing the radical separation (verse 12).

6. The parent-child relationship and parental pity form an analogy by which to understand divine love. It should be noted that such pity is granted to those fearing (obeying the will of) God (verse 13; note verses 17-18). The human condition helps incline God to mercy: God knows the weakness of the human condition: people's dusty origin and their dusty destiny (verse 14).

II Corinthians 3:1-6

As is the case with much of Second Corinthians, today's epistolary lesson is written in response to charges made against Paul by his rivals. One of their complaints was that Paul engaged in excessive self-commendation. At issue may have been the exceptional nature of Paul's apostolic call, and hence the legitimacy of his apostolic credentials.

Unlike the original apostolic circle, he could not claim to

have been with Jesus, or to have been directly commissioned by the historical Jesus. Instead, his apostleship was exceptional (I Cor. 15:8-9). We can imagine that without this historical link with Jesus and the apostolic circle, Paul could be perceived as one whose credentials were self-generated. Given the strength of his personality, we can also imagine his detractors accusing him of preaching himself rather than the gospel. Thus he must insist that he does not preach himself (as Lord), but Christ Jesus as Lord (II Cor. 4:5).

Another factor leading to this perception may have had to do with his theology of preaching as reenactment of the cross. So closely did he identify his apostolic sufferings with the suffering of Christ that he often rehearsed what he had to endure as part of the message he preached (cf. I Cor. 4:9-13; also II Cor. 6:4-10; 11:23-29).

Whatever the reasons for this adverse perception of Paul, we find him explaining the nature of authentic apostolic existence. He contrasts himself with his opponents "who commend themselves" by engaging in games of oneupmanship (II Cor. 10:12). What was especially painful to Paul is that they had gained an entrance within the Corinthian church and had begun to win the favor of those for whom he felt a divine jealousy (II Cor. 11:2, 4). In the end, Paul insists, what matters is not whether we approve of our own actions but whether the Lord does (II Cor. 10:18). Consequently, every effort to get a hearing for the gospel must be anchored in the proper understanding of ministry. If we commend ourselves, it must be as "servants of Christ," nothing more, nothing less (II Cor. 6:4). Moreover, when we seek to gain favor for the sake of the gospel, it must be "by the open statement of the truth" (II Cor. 4:2). It cannot be by the use of cunning, underhanded methods that can only flourish when hidden from view (II Cor. 4:2). What we do, we do "in the sight of God" (II Cor. 4:2). Paul is calling here for a form of ministerial authentication that operates in the public arena.

One way to be commended was through the well-established practice of using letters of recommendation. When the new convert Apollos sought to go to Achaia in order to preach, the brethren first wrote letters of recommendation on his behalf (Acts 18:27). Even Paul himself wrote letters of recommendation for "Phoebe, a deaconness of the church at Cenchreae" (Rom. 16:1-2) and Mark the cousin of Barnabas (Col. 4:10). Apparently, Paul's opponents had employed this same practice to gain an entrance within the church. But the last thing he needed in order to document his standing with the Corinthian church was letters of recommendation, either to them or from them (verse 2). This might have been acceptable had he been unknown to them, but he was their "father . . . through the gospel" (I Cor. 4:15).

Consequently, they themselves were his letter of recommendation (verse 2). Whether Paul conceives of these letters as written on the Corinthians' hearts ("your hearts," RSV) or on the hearts of Paul himself and his co-workers ("our hearts," NEB, JB, NIV) is a disputed textual point. Probably the latter, since it makes more sense of the text to think of the church's own existence and reputation as what would have been "known and read by all men" (verse 2). It was, after all, the church who remained in the apostle's heart (II Cor. 7:2). They were the seal of his apostleship (I Cor. 9:2). Whether he had anything to commend him depended upon whether the church had anything to commend it. The litmus paper test of the minister's work is the minister's church. The results of ministry either commend or condemn the minister.

But more is involved here than the notion that the church is a mirror image of the minister. They were to see themselves as "a letter from Christ delivered by us, written not with ink but with the Spirit of the living God, not on tablets of stone but on tablets of human hearts" (verse 3). After all, the church was not self-generated, nor was it even generated as an act of apostolic prowess. It was a "church of God" (II Cor. 1:1) established in Christ (II Cor. 1:21). Nor had the work of God in Christ been inscribed on hearts of stone as was the case with the tablets of testimony God gave Moses (Exod. 31:18; 32:15-16; Deut. 9:10). Rather, what had been promised by God through the prophets had now come to pass: the human heart was the place where the imprint of God's Spirit could be traced (Ezek. 11:19; 36:26; cf. Jer. 31:33; also Prov. 7:3). The work of God is now penciled in the heart of those to whom God's Spirit had been given as a guarantee (II Cor. 1:22).

177

Seen this way, the minister is not the prime actor in God's work among churches. It is not the minister's sufficiency, or lack of it, that legitimates this process: "our sufficiency is of God" (verse 5, KJV). Consequently, the minister's confidence is not self-generated; it is derived. It occurs "through Christ toward God" (verse 4).

The mention of "tablets of stone" (verse 3) prompts Paul to introduce the notion of the "new covenant" (verse 6; cf. Jer. 31:31). Fundamental to his discussion is the distinction between "letter" and "spirit" (verse 6). What is written in letters of the alphabet, whether with a pen on papyrus or with the finger of God on stone tablets, is said to "kill." This doubtless refers to Paul's conviction that the law written on stone produced despair and finally death (Rom. 3:9-20; 7:13). In the end, the law was incapable of giving life (Gal. 3:21-22). It is the Spirit, finally, who can give life (Rom. 8:6, 11; cf. I Cor. 15:45).

As homiletical possibilities, the preacher may wish to explore the question of what constitutes authentic ministry. In doing so, one could examine the relationship between the minister and the church. But today's text would insist that this relationship is never merely a matter of human engineering; it must rather be construed primarily as an arena in which God is at work—through the minister to be sure, but not as the primary agent whose sufficiency and confidence are self-generated.

The distinction between letter and spirit also holds germinal possibilities. Our inclination to "have it in writing," as noble as it is and as secure as it makes us feel, may serve as a reminder that a contract, however properly drawn up and however precise, is only as good as the human hearts within which it finally has to be negotiated.

Mark 2:18-22

Mark 2:18-22 (Matt. 9:14-17; Luke 5:33-39) is the record of the third of five controversy stories in the section 2:1–3:6. (For comments on this section see last Sunday's lesson.) Our lesson for today consists of two parts: verses 18-20 and verses 21-22.

It is quite clear that the controversy over fasting has been framed by Mark so as to address the church. The question put to Jesus was not, "Why do you not fast?" but, "Why do your disciples not fast?" In other words, Mark presents a church issue which was worked out in relation to two religious groups with which the church shared a common heritage: the Pharisees and the followers of John the Baptist (verse 18). The Pharisees were required to fast on the Day of Atonement and in times of special need, but it was quite common to do voluntary fasting in the practice of piety. The followers of John were imitating their leader in their fasting, "for John came neither eating nor drinking" (Matt. 11:18). Jesus, even though he fasted in the desert of temptation (Matt. 4:2), "came eating and drinking," drawing the criticism that he was a glutton and a drunkard (Matt. 11:19).

According to Mark, the issue is not whether or not to fast. After all, Jesus says, "The days will come, when the bridegroom is taken away from them, and then they will fast in that day" (verse 20). If "that day" refers to Jesus' death, then the text instructs Jesus' followers that during Jesus' life fasting was not appropriate, but it would be appropriate upon Jesus' departure. Fasting, in other words, was to be joined to some occasions but not to all. During his trials alone in the desert, Jesus fasted, but not during his work of healing and preaching the Good News of the kingdom of God. One does not fast at a party. There is a time to fast and there is a time to kill the fatted calf. The coming of Jesus and the joyful news of the kingdom's arrival were radically new, demanding forms of expression appropriate to this New Age.

Conversely, continuous banqueting would violate certain seasons of the soul and critical moments in the life of the church. As Jesus predicted, the days came for fasting. The church at Antioch fasted prior to the sending out of Barnabas and Saul (Acts 13:2-3). The appointing of elders for every church was done with prayer and fasting (Acts 14:23). According to Matthew, fasting along with prayer and alms were the staples in the practice of Christian piety (6:1-6, 16-18). In fact, Matthew's expression, "when you fast," assumes the practice is well in place and the instruction needed is in the area of genuineness, without hypocrisy. As with all practices that become regularized, however sincere and prayerfully motivated at the outset, the dangers of empty routine and false display are never far away. One detects, for example, a hollow ring in the instruction given in an early Christian document: fast on Wednesday and Friday and not on Monday and Thursday as the hypocrites do (*Didache* 8:1). It is the endless business of the church to keep its words and acts alive, appropriate, and toward God.

The second part of our lesson, verses 21-22, consists of proverbs about garments and wineskins. These proverbs, as is true of most proverbs, give themselves to multiple applications. In their present location in Mark they refer to the arrival of something so vital and new that it cannot be contained in the old rituals and forms of piety. It is important to notice that in these verses Mark is not attacking the old. There is concern expressed about the loss of the old garment and the old wineskin just as there is about the loss of the new. Each has its integrity, and it would be a violation of both to treat the Christian faith as a compromise of the old and the new, a synthesis of the two at the level of lowest common denominators. No one gains by pretending Hanukkah is Christmas or that Christmas is Hanukkah. To try fasting at a party is to make a display of fasting and to wreck the party. Like so much of life, the key is very often in the timing.

Last Sunday After Epiphany (Transfiguration)

II Kings 2:1-12a; Psalm 50:1-6; II Corinthians 4:3-6; Mark 9:2-9

The last Sunday after Epiphany always centers on the Transfiguration, and the texts for today dramatically point to the pivotal event in the ministry of Jesus. The Gospel record is Mark's brief but forceful account, and it is the Gospel text that attracts to itself the other readings. Elijah appears with Jesus on the mountain; II Kings 2 tells of Elijah's glorious ascent to heaven. Psalm 50 speaks of the appearance of God attended by fire and storm. And Paul in II Corinthians 4 uses the imagery of Old Testament theophanies and of the Transfiguration to speak of God's presence in Christ and of Christ's presence in us, veiled in flesh to be sure, but glorious nonetheless.

II Kings 2:1-12*a*

The selection of this Old Testament text for Transfiguration Sunday is based on the fact that Elijah appears in the narrative of Jesus' Transfiguration and that the story of Elijah's ascension to heaven forms an analogous parallel to the ultimate ascension and glorification of Jesus which are anticipated in the Transfiguration.

In this narrative, three features help structure the story and increase the tension of the plot. There is, first of all, the travel itinerary of Elijah and Elisha. The two begin their journey at Gilgal, where the Hebrews first made camp after crossing the Jordan River (Josh. 5:1-9). Then they progress to Bethel, one of the sacred temple sites of Israel, the place where the national shrine was constructed for the Northern Kingdom (I Kings 12:26-29). From Bethel, the two return to Jericho, the site of the Hebrews' first triumph on the western side of the

Jordan (Josh. 6). They next go to the Jordan River which the Hebrews earlier crossed in miraculous fashion (Josh. 3:14-17). Finally, the journey carries the men across the Jordan after Elijah parts the water with his mantle. Why the storyteller structured his story around these geographical points remains uncertain. Perhaps the ancient hearer would have thought that one of these great and famous sites would be the place of departure but one by one they are bypassed. It is as if Elijah conducts a miniature tour of the Land of Promise before departing this world from a location "beyond the Jordan."

A second feature in the story is the persistent fidelity and loyalty of Elisha who faithfully follows his master without leaving his presence. Elisha is the true disciple. The story of Elijah's first meeting with Elisha is a paradigm of the true follower (I Kings 19:19-21). In his call, Elisha initially hesitates to follow Elijah begging first to bid farewell to his family. Elijah would have none of this. To show that he was forsaking the past and "burning his bridges behind him," Elisha slaughtered his yoke of twelve oxen, his means of livelihood, and offered them up as a feast for the people. In II Kings 2:1-12a, Elisha has the option of ceasing to follow Elijah wherever he goes, but still he follows loyally.

A third feature of the story is the unveiled mystery of Elijah's departure. It is an open secret since all the "sons of the prophets" (members of the prophetic guilds) remind Elisha that the time of his master's departure is near. The departure is certain, only the circumstances and the place remain uncertain. (Note a similar emphasis on the uncertainty and questioning about Jesus' "departure" in Mark's account of the Transfiguration.)

The narrative of Elijah's departure does not conclude before Elisha requests to be the true successor of his master, only he wishes to possess double the spirit of Elijah. One requirement is placed on Elisha: he must witness, actually see, the departure of his master. The text is careful to note that this occurred. At Elijah's departure, Elisha calls to him with two honorific titles: "father" out of respect for his position, age, and authority; and "the chariots of Israel and its horsemen" to indicate the importance of Elijah in the earlier history of Israel—he was more powerful than the instruments of war.

This narrative, like the accounts of the Transfiguration, is filled with mystery, awe, miracle, and legend. All of these factors in their own way were used by the ancients to show that a person had unusual, superhuman qualities. Such persons are those in whose very existence dwells the quality and power of the other world.

Psalm 50:1-6

These opening verses of the psalm form part of a call to worship which constitute an affirmation of the coming of Yahweh to judge the people. The remainder of the psalm is composed of speeches of Yahweh to the worshipers placing them under judgment and condemnation. This psalm thus appears clearly to have been part of a liturgy of judgment carried out in the context of worship, perhaps a service of covenant renewal or of national lamentation. Some officiating priest perhaps spoke verses 1-6 and a prophet proclaimed the judgment of God in the remainder of the psalm.

This psalm, like the Transfiguration scene, speaks of the presence of awesome phenomena as attendant upon the coming of God—devouring fire and mighty tempest. Such descriptions were at home in speech about Yahweh's appearance in theophanies and especially about the theophany at Sinai (Exod. 19:16-19). Just as God appeared at Sinai when the law was given with the accompaniment of unusual phenomena so in similar terminology Psalm 50 describes the appearance of the Deity to judge the people.

The psalm opens with a piling up of divine names—El ("Mighty One"), Elohim ("God"), Yahweh ("the Lord"). This threefold ascription of names, which stresses the honorific power of the divine, is followerd by a threefold summons to assemble for judgment. God summons the earth (verse 1), then the heavens and the earth (verse 4), and finally "my faithful ones" or the members of the covenant community. The heavens and the earth are to appear as witnesses to the proclamation of judgment that follows since they, as permanent features of the world, are also witnesses to the initial giving of the law and the demands for obedience.

The significant points of connection between this reading from the psalm and the Transfiguration of Jesus are the reference to God's shining forth (verse 2) and the statement that God is judge (verse 6). In Psalm 50, God calls and speaks from the heavens. In the Transfiguration, God speaks from the cloud. In addition, God's appearance and Jesus' Transfiguration are presented with unusual features, features that call for a response of awe in the presence of the other world.

II Corinthians 4:3-6

These words from Paul clearly echo themes found in Mark's account of the Transfiguration of Jesus. Perhaps most striking is the recurrent theme of "light" which is, of course, central to the Transfiguration story itself. As the Gospel account stresses the dazzling radiance of Christ, flanked by Moses and Elijah, so does Paul focus attention on the "light of the gospel of the glory of Christ, who is the likeness of God" (verse 4). Rather than drawing his imagery from the Sinai theophany, as does the Transfiguration story, Paul is informed by another part of the biblical witness—the Old Testament account of creation. Directly quoting Genesis 1:3, Paul says that the God who said, "Let light shine out of darkness," is also the God who brought light to the Christian's heart by giving "the light of the knowledge of the glory of God in the face of Christ" (verse 6).

The Sinai theophany has already figured centrally in Paul's remarks in chapter 3, where he insisted that the "glory" or "splendor" of Christ can now be viewed directly "with unveiled face" (II Cor. 3:18). Those whose confidence is "through Christ toward God" find themselves being gradually transformed into his likeness as they acquire this dazzling glory of the Lord.

Paul fully recognizes that for some, his gospel is veiled (verse 3). Blinded by the "god of this world," unbelievers find themselves in a position analogous to the disciples in the Transfiguration story who, at first, were unable to see the transfigured Christ. However, with the voice from heaven acclaiming him "the beloved son," and with the injunction that they are now to "listen to him," God's revelation in Christ is placed in the public domain.

The verses immediately preceding today's text indicate that Paul had been accused by his opponents in Corinth of obstructing the message of Christ in some way. Paul insists, however, that his methods of preaching were fully compatible with the nature of the gospel itself. He refrained from the use of rhetorical devices or underhanded methods and rather insisted that his gospel could in no way be understood as oriented toward himself. The content of his gospel is not himself (verse 5), but the crucified Christ. He made a considered effort to keep himself in a servant role as minister of the gospel of Christ (verse 5b).

Nevertheless, Paul acknowledges that the gospel cannot be preached apart from the human personality. As he states in the following remarks, the gospel must ultimately be mediated through "earthen vessels" (verse 7), and because of this intrinsic human dimension of the gospel, he makes sure that his own life is "cruciform" in order adequately to convey the central message of the crucified Christ (verses 11-12).

Paul's use of the creation story, with its emphasis on God's power to give light to the world in the creative act of making light shine out of darkness, is carried through even further in II Corinthians 5 where he speaks of the "new creation." The Christ-event itself is viewed as a second creation in the sense that the whole cosmos is reordered, and the one who is "in Christ" comes to share in this newly created eschatological reality. Accordingly, through the Christ-event it may be said that God gave light to the world once again, in a much more spectacular sense. Now, however, as the new age has dawned, it is the "face of Christ" (verse 6) that serves as the source of this dazzling radiance.

It is worth noting that as Paul's remarks continue in verses 7-12, they resemble in many senses the nature of Jesus' instructions to his disciples after the Transfiguration in the Gospel account. There, he begins to speak of the necessity of his death and suffering, even as does Paul in verses 7-12. It might be said that the Epiphany of Christ (note "manifested" in verse 11) takes its most legitimate form within our mortal flesh as we reenact the suffering and death of Christ, as did Paul.

Mark 9:2-9

On this closing Sunday of Epiphany we will consider Mark's major contribution to this season, the story of the Transfiguration of Jesus (9:2-9). Here Mark gathers up in a single event what the Fourth Evangelist scatters throughout his Gospel: the glory of Christ. This is, in the dramatic sense, the scene of recognition, the moment in which the reader and a chosen few present are permitted to see the principal character in full glory. The Transfiguration recalls the baptism of Jesus with the voice from heaven and the identity of Jesus as God's Son. Here, however, the voice speaks to the disciples, not to Jesus. Transfiguration also anticipates the resurrection, although there is in Mark no actual resurrection appearance (16:1-8). But this story, located almost exactly at the midpoint of the Gospel, has its own structure and in Mark's purpose, its own message. Let us look at the text internally and then seek to understand the point of the story in Mark's theology.

Quite clearly Mark 9:2-9 is patterned after the stories of Moses' experiences of God on Mt. Sinai. One would do well to read Exodus 24 and 34 in preparation for understanding the text. All the elements of Mark's account are there: the six days of waiting, the cloud, the glory, the voice, the descent from the mountain. Moses' face shone due to his experience in the presence of God. Exodus also describes the making of the tent of meeting. Peter, James, and John as the inner circle invited to share special experiences are frequently mentioned in Mark (5:37; 13:3; 14:33). As to the appearance of Elijah and Moses, these two had come to be associated with the Messianic Age in both Judaism and Christianity (Mal. 4:1-6; Deut. 18:15-18; Rev. 11:3ff.). That they appear with Jesus says that the anticipated Messiah and the end-time are fulfilled in

Jesus. That they disappear, leaving only Jesus, says that the old is ended, the new has come. As at the baptism, Jesus does not act or speak; God acts and God speaks concerning Jesus. And the message of the occasion is for Jesus' followers. They do not understand the event, being afraid and confused. Peter's fumbling effort to honor and preserve the moment is met with silence. Therefore, they are enjoined to be silent about the experience until after the resurrection (verse 9). They are not ready to be witnesses to Jesus' messianic role nor are their auditors ready to hear it. Apart from the cross the full story cannot be told.

What, then, is Mark saying in this account? Gospel writers reveal their intent either in how a story is told or in when a story is told; that is, where it is located in the narrative. It is the latter clue that is most helpful here. The Transfiguration is located in the central section of Mark 8:22–10:52. This section opens with the healing of a blind man and ends with the healing of a blind man. In between, however, the disciples remain blind. Jesus three times predicts his death (8:31; 9:31; 10:33-34), but on each occasion the disciples amply demonstrate their inability to accept a cross and death as being anything but a contradiction of all that Messiah and kingdom mean. Peter's confession has the right words but the wrong meaning (8:29-30). After all, how can persons who have lived with a motto, "When the Messiah comes, there will be no misery," understand suffering and death as kingdom experiences? And so between the first announcement of his passion and the passion itself comes the Transfiguration. Disciples who had been hearing death talk are given a glimpse of who Jesus really is. A corner of the curtain is lifted and they are permitted to see and hear for a moment. But they miss it really. Simon Peter, who had interrupted Jesus at prayer to call him back on stage before an applauding crowd (1:35-38), now wants to perpetuate this marvelous moment. Here is the real glory, without suffering, without death. Jesus' silence before Peter's offer says to him and to all followers that glimpses of the glorious future are permitted, but not possession of that future. That future, like the past, is not the proper dwelling place for the church. For these disciples, and all who follow, there is one more mountain to climb: Golgotha.

Some readers of Mark position themselves over against the disciples, critical of them in their confusion, doubt, and cowardice. Others identify with the disciples and bow over this text, indicted, penitent, and forgiven.

Holy Name of Jesus; Solemnity of Mary, Mother of God, January 1

Numbers 6:22-27; Psalm 67; Galatians 4:4-7 or Philippians 2:9-13; Luke 2:15-21

Celebrating the beginning of the new year on January 1 goes back to the mid-first century B.C., when Julius Caesar restructured the civil calendar. Prior to that time, March 1 marked the beginning of the new year. From the outset, it was a festive celebration that easily gave way to excesses of various kinds. In response, the Roman church called on Christians to open the new year with prayer, fasting, and penitential devotions. Another way to provide an alternative to raucous festivals was to designate January 1 as a time for honoring Mary the Mother of God. In the Roman calendar the day was designated *Natale Sanctae Mariae*, the Feast of Saint Mary.

Even though the particular emphasis given to January 1 has shifted through the centuries, in modern times, and especially in the Roman church, this day has received a dual emphasis. First, it is a time to recall the naming of Jesus, hence the designation the "Holy Name of Jesus." This aspect of its celebration is closely related to the custom, going back at least to the sixth century, of celebrating the Feast of the Circumcision of the Lord on this day. Second, it is an occasion for commemorating Mary, hence the designation the "Solemnity of Mary, Mother of God."

The selection of readings for this day echoes these themes. The Old Testament reading is chosen because of its emphasis on the bestowal of the Divine Name on the people Israel. Psalm 67 closely parallels Numbers 6:22-27 in the form of the blessing it contains. The epistolary readings in different ways pick up on both themes: the Galatians passage embodies a pre-Pauline tradition in which Christ is confessed as one "born of woman, born under the law," while the Philippians reading lays stress on the exalted name that God bestowed on the risen Lord. The Gospel text, of course, combines both themes: the central role of Mary as the one who pondered the divine mystery in her heart and the circumcision of Jesus as the occasion when he received the holy name.

Numbers 6:22-27

Within the Pentateuch as a whole, Numbers 6:22-27 is part of the laws given through Moses at Mount Sinai. The section of which it is a part began with Exodus 19 and will end in Numbers 10. In terms of literary source, this unit like most of the laws from Sinai from Exodus 25 to Numbers 10, comes from the Priestly Writer (sixth century B.C.). Specifically, the stress on the priesthood of the sons of Aaron (6:23) reveals that writer's point of view. However, in the great body of legislation this passage stands out for its poetic style, suggesting that the blessing itself is much older than the source in which it is found. Its style and content clearly reflect its repeated cultic use.

The unit consists of the Aaronic blessing surrounded by a brief narrative framework. The narrative (6:22) simply but significantly indicates that what follows is a divine speech to Moses. The benediction as a prayer for God's blessing was itself a gift from God. The speech instructs Moses to tell Aaron and his sons—that is, all future priests in the line, down to the writer's day—to bless the people of Israel, it gives them the words of the blessing, and then (6:27) it states the meaning of the act of blessing.

The blessing contains three sentences, each with two parts and each one longer than the one before. Every sentence begins with the divine name, Yahweh, followed by verbal forms that indicate wish or hope, e.g., "*May* the Lord bless you. . ." (GNB). They are then prayers for the well-being of those addressed. Since the form of address is second person singular, the blessing may apply equally to individuals or to a group. The contents concern God's protection (verse 24), gracious care (verse 25), and gift of peace. "Peace" is a comprehensive term, a fitting greeting, that includes wholeness. Priests are to pronounce the blessing but, as verse 27 expressly states, the Lord is the one who blesses.

What does it mean that by pronouncing the blessing the sons of Aaron thus put the divine name upon Israel? One hardly needs to stress the importance of names in the Old Testament. Abram and Sarai were given with the covenant new names (Gen. 17). After struggling through the night, Jacob was given the new name Israel, but the one with whom he struggled would not reveal his name, for in the name is power (Gen. 32:27-29). Yahweh was to be worshiped at the place which he would choose "to put his name" (Deut. 12:5). To put the name of the Lord over the people of Israel is to indicate that others know them, and they know themselves by that name. They are thereby identified with this God, and this God is identified with them.

Psalm 67

This psalm presents the reader or interpreter with what appears to be a twofold dialectic. On the one hand, the psalm is a prayer or speech to the Deity (verses 2-5) and yet it contains speech about God (verses 1, 6-7). In addition, the psalm apparently offers thanks for blessings already received (verses 6-7) and yet requests blessing from God (verses 1-5). The psalm thus has some of the characteristics of a lament (petitions for blessing) and of a thanksgiving.

The tension in the psalm can also be seen in its stress on both the particular (the people of Israel; the "us" of the psalm) and the universal (the nations; the peoples of the world). The request for blessing upon the more restricted community, that is, the "us" of verses 1, 6, and 7, has as its ultimate goal, the recognition of God by foreigners and the praise of the nations.

The analogies between this psalm and Christmas, holy family, and Mary the mother of Jesus might be seen as the following. The birth of a child has very specific, very limited connotations. The child is very particular: the particular

191

offspring of a particular locale. The birth is always to a particular "us." Yet the birth of Jesus is proclaimed as possessing universal ramifications that reach out to the nations and the peoples of the world. The Incarnation is at once a most particular and universal event. At the same time, a birth is a blessing and an occasion for thanks (verses 6-7) and yet it looks forward to the future, to the expectation and intercession of blessings to come.

Galatians 4:4-7

"Born of woman, born under the law." These few words are as close as Paul comes to providing a birth and infancy narrative of Jesus. Yet, for all their remarkable compactness, they capture the essence of Luke's birth narrative. "Born of woman" naturally applies to Mary's giving birth to the Son of God, and it is this phrase that especially commends this epistolary lection for the celebration of New Year's Day as the "Solemnity of Mary, Mother of God." Some scholars believe that the phrase is pre-Pauline, and thus stems from the very earliest stages of primitive Christianity. If it is part of a creedal statement, we can see that quite early on Mary was the object of early Christian confession.

If "born of woman" underscores the humanity of Jesus, "born under the law" underscores his Jewishness. For Paul, this had special significance, since he is concerned to show that precisely because Jesus lived under the Mosaic law he was able to redeem us from the bondage of the law. What Paul says here in shorthand, Luke portrays in narrative form: Jesus circumcised according to the prescription of the Law (Luke 2:21) and brought to the temple for the rite of consecration (Luke 2:22-38). He is the son of parents loyally devoted to life according to the Law of Moses (Luke 2:39-51). Just as the first phrase links the epistolary text with the celebration of Mary as the Mother of God, so does this second phrase link directly with the circumcision and naming of Jesus (Luke 2:21).

Homiletically, these two motifs might be explored by showing how the devotion of Mary, as depicted in the Gospel reading, related to the devotion of Jesus. Both have in

192

common their loyalty to the law of God. We are told that she and Joseph were scrupulously loyal, performing "everything according to the law of the Lord" (Luke 2:39). In the same breath, Jesus is portrayed in terms reminiscent of Samuel, the faithful servant of God (I Sam. 3:19). It would be possible to trace the Lukan portrait of Mary, especially noting her favorable status (in contrast to the Markan portrait) as among those "who hear the word of God and do it" (Luke 8:19-21).

Like mother, like son.

Philippians 2:9-13

If one chooses the Holy Name of Jesus as the focus of attention on New Year's Day, this will be the more appropriate epistolary text. For those who know that verses 9-11 comprise the second stanza of the Christ-hymn that Paul quotes here, it may appear odd to begin the reading at verse 9. But certainly that part of the hymn draws our attention to God's bestowal of the divine name on Jesus.

If this epistolary text is chosen, it provides a strong counterpart to the Gospel reading (Luke 2:15-21), where the name given to the Son of God, according to the angel's prescription, is "Jesus" (Luke 1:31). By contrast, in the epistolary reading the "name which is above every name" (verse 9) is "Lord" (cf. I Thess. 1:1). This is the name bestowed on Jesus because of his resurrection (Rom. 1:4); or, in the words of our passage, because "God has highly exalted him" (verse 9). To be sure, it is the "name of Jesus" before which the universe bows in submission, but the heart of the confession is that "Jesus Christ is Lord." We can begin to see the true significance of this ascription if we remember that in the Greek Old Testament Yahweh was commonly designated as Lord. Thus, for Christians to give Jesus this title was to ascribe him a status normally reserved for Israel's God, Yahweh.

The sequel to this part of the Christ-hymn is well worth exploring in a New Year's Day setting, because it spells out the implications of confessing and submitting to the divine name of Jesus Christ the Lord. Submission to the name implies submissive obedience which is worked out in salvation. It is not, however, the work that we do but the work that God does within us that brings about such obedience. We are reminded that "fear and trembling" accompany God's saving work within us. Not that we become feckless and craven before a vindictive, bloodthirsty God, but that we respect the exalted status and universal dominion of the One we confess as Lord. Such a perspective creates within us a healthy respect for the numinous and holy that prevents us from confessing the name of Jesus blithely and unthinkingly. This day is, after all, a celebration of the *Holy* Name of Jesus. It may be well to call the church to recover this sacred dimension as it launches into a new year.

Luke 2:15-21

Today we return to a portion of the Christmas story, but since the special nature of this service provides the reason for this return, it is appropriate that the nature and purpose of the service guide the approach to the text. Because attention may be focused on Mary's response to the events which surround her child or on the service of naming the child, these two approaches to the text offer themselves, plus a third which will be suggested at the close of these comments.

To give special attention to Mary would be to do no more than Luke himself has done. If Protestants think the Roman Catholic tradition has made too much of her, they could reasonably be charged with a neglect of her. While Luke is more attentive to women in general than are the other Evangelists (note, for example, 8:1-3; 23:27-31; 23:55; 24:10; Acts 1:14), his portrayal of Mary is noticeably distinct. There is in Luke, we remind ourselves, the episode of a woman in a crowd shouting to Jesus, "Blessed is the womb that bore you, and the breasts that you sucked!" to whom Jesus responded, "Blessed rather are those who hear the word of God and keep it!" (11:27-28). But upon reflection, Jesus' response is not a distancing from Mary but an embrace of her on the very grounds on which Luke consistently presents her as blessed: she received and obeyed the word of God. From the beginning, in response to the annunciation by the messenger Gabriel, Mary's relation to all that followed was clear:

"Behold, I am the handmaid of the Lord; let it be to me according to your word" (1:38). Elizabeth eulogized Mary as one who believed in God's faithfulness in fulfilling promises (1:45). Mary's own song reflects strong confidence and hope in God (1:46-55). She did not always understand what was said about her child, whether by shepherds (2:19) or by old Simeon at the temple (2:33). Neither did she understand the words and behavior of her son at age twelve (2:48-51). Even so, she kept all these things in her heart (2:19, 51), and she was found among those in Jerusalem waiting in prayer for the Holy Spirit promised by her risen son (Acts 1:5, 14).

If today's service attends primarily to the naming of Jesus, only verse 21 pertains to it. However, the brevity of the text should not be taken as brevity of meaning. First of all, the circumcision and naming of Jesus was according to the law (Lev. 12:3). Luke is careful to point out that the entire life of Jesus from birth, circumcision, dedication, Passover observance at age twelve, regular synagogue attendance, and even through his death and resurrection, was according to the Law of Moses as well as a fulfillment of the Prophets and the Psalms. Jesus is the true Israelite. Second, the naming confirmed the promise of the messenger from God and demonstrated the faith of Mary and Joseph in that promise (1:31; 2:21). And finally, the name itself was significant. Jesus, or Joshua, meant "one who saves." Such was his description to the shepherds in the field (2:11), and so he was and is, as Matthew also testifies (1:21).

However, the preacher may prefer to return to the text as a story and enjoy again its beauty and insight. The story line is simple: the shepherds come to Bethlehem, find Mary, Joseph, and the baby, relate their extraordinary experience, causing all who heard to wonder, and then return to their flocks, glorifying and praising God. They alone experienced both the shining glory and the mangered baby, the angel's revelation and the mother's whispers, the heavenly choir and the stabled animals. Those present at the manger had only the baby; Mary and Joseph had only the baby. But now they had the witness of the shepherds about the baby, and it is that witness which generates wondering, pondering, believing, and praising God.

195

Presentation, February 2

Malachi 3:1-4; Psalm 84 or 24:7-10; Hebrews 2:14-18;
Luke 2:22-40

This day is the celebration of the event reported in the Gospel reading, the presentation of Jesus in the temple in Jerusalem in accordance with Jewish law. Either of the psalms is highly appropriate, for both enable the church at worship to recreate the scene at the temple. Psalm 84 is a pilgrim hymn in praise of Zion and Psalm 24:7-10 is an entrance liturgy that praises the king of glory. The christological reflections in Hebrews 2:14-18 show a fully human Lord as high priest in service of God. Malachi 3:1-4 is the promise of a messenger of the covenant who will come like a "refiner's fire," after which the offerings—such as those mentioned in the Gospel—will be acceptable to God.

Malachi 3:1-4

For comments on the Old Testament lesson see the discussion of the readings for the Second Sunday of Advent, Year C.

Psalm 84

The two psalms selected for reading in celebration of Jesus' presentation at the temple are both concerned with devotion to the temple. Psalm 84 may have been once used in conjunction with making a pilgrimage to Jerusalem at festival time, although verse 9 seems to suggest it was used by the king. Psalm 24 contains words spoken at the time when pilgrims entered the sanctuary precincts.

Psalm 84:5-7 probably talks about the route to Zion taken by pilgrims as they made their way along the roads to the city. At the time of fall festival, some of the early autumn rains may already have fallen reviving the parched land. "Strength to strength" could be translated "stronghold to stronghold," that is, the people move from one village outpost to another.

The piety of the worshiper and the psalm composer can be seen in various ways in the text. One way of analyzing the materials is to note the three groups whom the writer declares "blessed" (or "happy" which is a better translation of the Hebrew word used in all three cases).

1. First, a happy company is the birds that dwell continuously in the temple (verses 3-4). The sparrows and swallows that nest in the sacred precincts have the advantage of constantly dwelling in the house of God where they can ever sing God's praise.

2. Happy are those who go on pilgrim to Jerusalem (verses 5-7). To visit the temple and Zion is to experience happiness and to see "the God of gods."

3. Happy are those who trust in God (verse 12) who find their confidence in him. Here we have a sort of generalizing pronouncement that moves beyond the specificity of temple piety.

Verse 10 may be taken as embodying the overall sentiment of the psalm: to visit the temple and worship in its courts were some of the supreme experiences for the ancient Hebrews.

Psalm 24:7-10

A litany of questions and responses make up the heart of Psalm 24. Originally written for use in temple worship, the following is an outline of the text: (1) hymn in praise of God (verses 1-2) probably sung by the whole congregation; (2) pilgrims' question about entering the sacred precincts of the temple mount (verse 3); (3) priestly response (verses 4-5); (4) pilgrims' reply to the priests (verse 6); and (5) a choral dialogue at the time the gates were opened allowing the people and God, represented by the ark, to enter (verses 7-10).

The reading of this psalm on Presentation Day results from the early church's identity of Jesus with the king of glory who enters the sanctuary.

Hebrews 2:14-18

At one time, especially in the Western church, this feast day was oriented toward Mary, and this was reflected in its name "Purification of the Blessed Virgin Mary." But because this appeared to threaten the doctrine of the sinlessness of Mary, in modern times the Roman church reverted to the more ancient understanding of the Eastern church which celebrated this day as the "Presentation of the Lord." This more nearly conformed to its various designations in the East: "Coming of the Son of God into the Temple" (Armenian); "Presentation of the Lord in the Temple" (Egyptian); "The Meeting of the Lord" (Byzantine). The shift in title reflects a shift in emphasis: it is intended to be a feast of the Lord and not a feast honoring Mary.

With this focus on the presentation of the Lord, which, according to scriptural prescription, took place forty days after his birth (Lev. 12:2-8), this feast day has an incarnational cast. Celebrated on February 2, the fortieth day after Christmas, it serves to mark the end of the Christmas season. While the Gospel reading provides an account of the Lukan story of the presentation of Jesus in the temple (Luke 2:22-40), the epistolary reading serves to anchor the redemptive work of Christ in his Incarnation. This text should not be forced in a false harmony with the Gospel reading, since each reflects a different theological interest. Nevertheless, there is a certain irony in the fact that the child who is presented in the temple "according to the law of Moses" finally becomes the merciful and faithful high priest officiating in the heavenly temple, making expiation for the sins of the people.

Several features of today's epistolary lection are worth noting.

First, the solidarity between Christ, "the one who sanctifies" and all humanity, "those who are sanctified" (verse 11). In the previous verses, several Old Testament texts are placed on the lips of Christ to show that he identifies completely with all of God's children (Ps. 22:22; Isa. 8:17-18). As such, he was born a member of the human family, sharing completely in our nature as "flesh and blood" (verse 14; Rom. 8:3, 29; Phil. 2:7). Just as it is the lot of every member of the human family to die, so did he experience death.

The effects of his death, however, were far from ordinary. For one thing, it was God "for whom and by whom all things exist" who made Jesus the "pioneer . . . perfect through suffering" (verse 10). In addition, through death he passed through the heavens and became the exalted Son of God (Heb. 4:14). Because his death was both uniquely exemplary and triumphant, he destroyed death as the stronghold of Satan (verse 14; John 12:31; Rom. 6:9; I Cor. 15:55; II Tim. 1:10; Rev. 12:10). In his death, he delivered "all those who through fear of death were subject to lifelong bondage" (verse 15). The incarnation of Christ eventually meant the freedom of all humanity from the fear of death.

Second, Christ as the merciful and faithful high priest (3:1; 4:14; 5:5, 10; 6:20; 7:26; 8:1; 9:11; 10:21). Because of his complete obedience, he demonstrated his true fidelity as the Son of God (5:8-9; cf. I Sam. 2:35). Because of his complete identification with the entire human family through his becoming "flesh and blood," he can be thoroughly sympathetic with the human condition. His own suffering and testing qualifies him to assist us in our sufferings and testing (verse 18; 5:2; cf. Matt. 4:1-11 and parallels; 26:36-46 and parallels).

In his role as high priest, Christ makes expiation for our sins (verse 17). His unique experience as one of God's earthly children makes it possible for him to plead in our behalf (5:1; Rom. 3:25; I John 2:2; 4:10; cf. Exod. 4:16).

Christ as a heavenly high priest, officiating in the heavenly temple and pleading in our behalf, can easily become a lofty image, far removed from the world we know and live in. Oddly enough, Christians have always found it easier to worship such an elevated Christ, enthroned high above the heavens. It is far more difficult for us to envision a Christ who became like us *in every respect* (verse 17). Yet today's epistolary text makes this unqualified claim about Christ who was concerned not with angels but with the descendants of Abraham (verse 16). Given a choice between the company of angels and the company of humans, Christ plumps for flesh and blood. Why shouldn't we?

Luke 2:22-40

The service of the Presentation of Jesus had its Gospel basis in Luke 2:22-40. This story and the one which follows (2:41-52) are found only in Luke.

Between the accounts of Jesus' birth and the beginning of his public life as an adult, Luke places three stories: the naming of Jesus at his circumcision (2:21), the presentation of Jesus in the temple (2:22-40), and the visit of Jesus to the temple at age twelve (2:41-52). All of them have as one clear purpose the demonstration that Jesus' family was careful to keep the Law of Moses and to observe all the practices appropriate to a pious, God-fearing Israelite family. Mary and Joseph were especially concerned to see that all the rites of passage for a firstborn male child were meticulously observed. If as an adult, as a teacher, preacher, and prophet Jesus was in tension with his tradition, it was not, says Luke, because the observance of that tradition was lacking in his life. On the contrary, Luke repeatedly points out that it was his religious tradition which nurtured in him the insights that brought him into conflict with flawed and hollow practices of that tradition.

The presentation story itself (2:22-40) consists of three parts: the framing story (verses 22-24, 39-40) into which are inserted the responses of Simeon (verses 25-35) and Anna (verses 36-38). The framing story itself makes three points vital for Luke's theology. First, the temple and Jerusalem are of central importance for Jesus and the early church (24:47-52; Acts 1:4; 2:46, and others). Second, the law of the Lord is observed (mentioned no less than five times in our text, verses 22, 23, 24, 27, 39). Luke here puts together two separate regulations: the purification of the mother after childbirth (Lev. 12:1-4), which required a sacrifice of a lamb and a pigeon except in hardship cases in which two pigeons or doves would suffice (Lev. 12:6-8), and the dedication of the firstborn son to God (Exod. 13:2, 12-16). The firstborn son could be redeemed for five shekels (Num. 18:15-16). This leads to the third point of the story: nothing is said by Luke about the child Jesus being redeemed from his belonging-to-God status under the law. He is, therefore, like Samuel who was dedicated to God, who grew in wisdom, in stature, and in God's favor (I Sam. 1–2), and who lived in the temple. Clearly the Samuel story lies back of the summary statements about Jesus' growth (verses 40, 52) and the account of Jesus' regarding the temple as his Father's house (verse 49).

The importance of Simeon (verses 25-35) is that he is a devout and righteous Jew, advanced in age, inspired by the Holy Spirit and looking for the consolation of Israel. The consolation of Israel was a way of referring to the messianic age, using liberally words and phrases from Isaiah 40–55. The Nunc Dimittis (verses 29-32) might have been an early Christian hymn familiar to the Lukan church. The consolation of Israel would not be easy or without cost. On the contrary, there would be opposition, the sword, and death (verses 34-35). But even so, Judaism, as represented in this old, righteous, Spirit-filled, hopeful man, a resident in the temple area, would be fulfilled in Jesus. With the arrival of Jesus, the old can depart in peace, giving way to the new.

The importance of Anna (verses 36-38) is that she is old (the Greek text is unclear as to whether she is eighty-four or has been a widow for eighty-four years), a prophetess, devout in the practice of prayer and fasting, and a resident in the temple who is looking for the redemption of Israel. Together with Simeon, Anna represents Israel seen in the most favorable light, and Israel, as portrayed in this old woman, sees in Jesus the redemption of Israel, gives thanks to God, and witnesses concerning Jesus to all who share Israel's hope. In other words, this is a portrait of the Israel that accepted Jesus. Those who rejected Jesus were those who misunderstood and misrepresented their own tradition and, therefore, were not capable of recognizing him as the continuation and the fulfillment of their own best memory and hope.

Scripture Reading Index

Table of Readings and Psalms

(Versification follows that of the Revised Standard Version)

		First Sunday of Advent	Second Sunday of Advent	Third Sunday of Advent	Fourth Sunday of Advent
A.	Lesson 1	Isaiah 2:1-5 Psalm 122	Isaiah 11:1-10 Psalm 72:1-8	Isaiah 35:1-10 Psalm 146:5-10	Isaiah 7:10-16 Psalm 24
	Lesson 2	Romans 13:11-14	Romans 15:4-13	James 5:7-10	Romans 1:1-7
	Gospel	Matthew 24:36-44	Matthew 3:1-12	Matthew 11:2-11	Matthew 1:18-25
B.	Lesson 1	Isaiah 63:16–64:8 Psalm 80:1-7	Isaiah 40:1-11 Psalm 85:8-13	Isaiah 61:1-4, 8-11 Luke 1:46*b*-55	II Samuel 7:8-16 Psalm 89:1-4, 19-24
	Lesson 2	I Corinthians 1:3-9	II Peter 3:8-15*a*	I Thessalonians 5:16-24	Romans 16:25-27
	Gospel	Mark 13:32-37	Mark 1:1-8	John 1:6-8, 19-28	Luke 1:26-38
C.	Lesson 1	Jeremiah 33:14-16 Psalm 25:1-10	Baruch 5:1-9 *or* Malachi 3:1-4 Psalm 126	Zephaniah 3:14-20 Isaiah 12:2-6	Micah 5:2-5*a* (5:1-4*a*) Psalm 80:1-7
	Lesson 2	I Thessalonians 3:9-13	Philippians 1:3-11	Philippians 4:4-9	Hebrews 10:5-10
	Gospel	Luke 21:25-36	Luke 3:1-6	Luke 3:7-18	Luke 1:39-55

	Christmas, First Proper (Christmas Eve/Day)*	Christmas, Second Proper (Additional Lessons for Christmas Day)	Christmas, Third Proper (Additional Lessons for Christmas Day)
A. Lesson 1	Isaiah 9:2-7	Isaiah 62:6-7, 10-12	Isaiah 52:7-10
	Psalm 96	Psalm 97	Psalm 98
Lesson 2	Titus 2:11-14	Titus 3:4-7	Hebrews 1:1-12
Gospel	Luke 2:1-20	Luke 2:8-20	John 1:1-14

*The readings from the second and third propers for Christmas may be used as alternatives for Christmas Day. If the third proper is not used on Christmas Day, it should be used at some service during the Christmas cycle because of the significance of John's Prologue.

		First Sunday After Christmas*	January 1—Holy Name of Jesus Solemnity of Mary, Mother of God	January 1 (when observed as New Year)	Second Sunday After Christmas**
A.	Lesson 1	Isaiah 63:7-9 Psalm 111	Numbers 6:22-27 Psalm 67	Deuteronomy 8:1-10 Psalm 117	Jeremiah 31:7-14 *or* Ecclesiasticus 24:1-4, 12-16 Psalm 147:12-20
	Lesson 2	Hebrews 2:10-18	Galatians 4:4-7 *or* Philippians 2:9-13	Revelation 21:1-6a	Ephesians 1:3-6, 15-18
	Gospel	Matthew 2:13-15, 19-23	Luke 2:15-21	Matthew 25:31-46	John 1:1-18
B.	Lesson 1	Isaiah 61:10-62:3 Psalm 111		Ecclesiastes 3:1-13 Psalm 8	
	Lesson 2	Galatians 4:4-7		Colossians 2:1-7	
	Gospel	Luke 2:22-40		Matthew 9:14-17	
C.	Lesson 1	I Samuel 2:18-20, 26 *or* Ecclesiasticus 3:3-7, 14-17 Psalm 111		Isaiah 49:1-10 Psalm 90:1-12	
	Lesson 2	Colossians 3:12-17		Ephesians 3:1-10	
	Gospel	Luke 2:41-52		Luke 14:16-24	

*Or the readings for Epiphany.

**Or the readings for Epiphany if not otherwise used.

	Epiphany	Baptism of the Lord (First Sunday After Epiphany)*	Second Sunday After Epiphany	Third Sunday After Epiphany	Fourth Sunday After Epiphany
A. Lesson 1	Isaiah 60:1-6 Psalm 72:1-14	Isaiah 42:1-9 Psalm 29	Isaiah 49:1-7 Psalm 40:1-11	Isaiah 9:1-4 Psalm 27:1-6	Micah 6:1-8 Psalm 37:1-11
Lesson 2	Ephesians 3:1-12	Acts 10:34-43	I Corinthians 1:1-9	I Corinthians 1:10-17	I Corinthians 1:18-31
Gospel	Matthew 2:1-12	Matthew 3:13-17	John 1:29-34	Matthew 4:12-23	Matthew 5:1-12
B. Lesson 1		Genesis 1:1-5 Psalm 29	I Samuel 3:1-10 (11-20) Psalm 63:1-8	Jonah 3:1-5, 10 Psalm 62:5-12	Deuteronomy 18:15-20 Psalm 111
Lesson 2		Acts 19:1-7	I Corinthians 6:12-20	I Corinthians 7:29-31 (32-35)	I Corinthians 8:1-13
Gospel		Mark 1:4-11	John 1:35-42	Mark 1:14-20	Mark 1:21-28
C. Lesson 1		Isaiah 61:1-4 Psalm 29	Isaiah 62:1-5 Psalm 36:5-10	Nehemiah 8:1-4a, 5-6, 8-10 Psalm 19:7-14	Jeremiah 1:4-10 Psalm 71:1-6
Lesson 2		Acts 8:14-17	I Corinthians 12:1-11	I Corinthians 12:12-30	I Corinthians 13:1-13
Gospel		Luke 3:15-17, 21-22	John 2:1-11	Luke 4:14-21	Luke 4:21-30

*In leap years, the number of Sundays after Epiphany will be the same as if Easter Day were one day later.

		Fifth Sunday After Epiphany	Sixth Sunday After Epiphany (Proper 1)	Seventh Sunday After Epiphany (Proper 2)	Eighth Sunday After Epiphany (Proper 3)	Last Sunday After Epiphany Transfiguration
A.	Lesson 1	Isaiah 58:3-9a Psalm 112:4-9	Deuteronomy 30:15-20 or Ecclesiasticus 15:15-20 Psalm 119:1-8	Isaiah 49:8-13 Psalm 62:5-12	Leviticus 19:1-2, 9-18 Psalm 119:33-40	Exodus 24:12-18 Psalm 2:6-11
	Lesson 2	I Corinthians 2:1-11	I Corinthians 3:1-9	I Corinthians 3:10-11, 16-23	I Corinthians 4:1-5	II Peter 1:16-21
	Gospel	Matthew 5:13-16	Matthew 5:17-26	Matthew 5:27-37	Matthew 5:38-48	Matthew 17:1-9
B.	Lesson 1	Job 7:1-7 Psalm 147:1-11	II Kings 5:1-14 Psalm 32	Isaiah 43:18-25 Psalm 41	Hosea 2:14-20 Psalm 103:1-13	II Kings 2:1-12a Psalm 50:1-6
	Lesson 2	I Corinthians 9:16-23	I Corinthians 9:24-27	II Corinthians 1:18-22	II Corinthians 3:1-6	II Corinthians 4:3-6
	Gospel	Mark 1:29-39	Mark 1:40-45	Mark 2:1-12	Mark 2:18-22	Mark 9:2-9
C.	Lesson 1	Isaiah 6:1-8 (9-13) Psalm 138	Jeremiah 17:5-10 Psalm 1	Genesis 45:3-11, 15 Psalm 37:1-11	Ecclesiasticus 27:4-7 or Isaiah 55:10-13 Psalm 92:1-4, 12-15	Exodus 34:29-35 Psalm 99
	Lesson 2	I Corinthians 15:1-11	I Corinthians 15:12-20	I Corinthians 15:35-38, 42-50	I Corinthians 15:51-58	II Corinthians 3:12-4:2
	Gospel	Luke 5:1-11	Luke 6:17-26	Luke 6:27-38	Luke 6:39-49	Luke 9:28-36

	Ash Wednesday	First Sunday of Lent	Second Sunday of Lent	Third Sunday of Lent	Fourth Sunday of Lent
A. Lesson 1	Joel 2:1-2, 12-17a	Genesis 2:4b-9, 15-17, 25—3:7	Genesis 12:1-4a (4b-8)	Exodus 17:3-7	I Samuel 16:1-13
Lesson 2	Psalm 51:1-12 II Corinthians 5:20b—6:2 (3-10)	Psalm 130 Romans 5:12-19	Psalm 33:18-22 Romans 4:1-5 (6-12), 13-17	Psalm 95 Romans 5:1-11	Psalm 23 Ephesians 5:8-14
Gospel	Matthew 6:1-6, 16-21	Matthew 4:1-11	John 3:1-17 *or* Matthew 17:1-9	John 4:5-26 (27-42)	John 9:1-41
B. Lesson 1		Genesis 9:8-17	Genesis 17:1-10, 15-19	Exodus 20:1-17	II Chronicles 36:14-23
Lesson 2		Psalm 25:1-10 I Peter 3:18-22	Psalm 105:1-11 Romans 4:16-25	Psalm 19:7-14 I Corinthians 1:22-25	Psalm 137:1-6 Ephesians 2:4-10
Gospel		Mark 1:9-15	Mark 8:31-38 *or* Mark 9:1-9	John 2:13-22	John 3:14-21
C. Lesson 1		Deuteronomy 26:1-11	Genesis 15:1-12, 17-18	Exodus 3:1-15	Joshua 5:9-12
Lesson 2		Psalm 91:9-16 Romans 10:8b-13	Psalm 127 Philippians 3:17—4:1	Psalm 103:1-13 I Corinthians 10:1-13	Psalm 34:1-8 II Corinthians 5:16-21
Gospel		Luke 4:1-13	Luke 13:31-35 *or* Luke 9:28-36	Luke 13:1-9	Luke 15:1-3, 11-32

	Fifth Sunday of Lent	Lent 6 when observed as Passion Sunday	Lent 6 when observed as Palm Sunday*
A. Lesson 1	Ezekiel 37:1-14 Psalm 116:1-9	Isaiah 50:4-9a Psalm 31:9-16	Isaiah 50:4-9a Psalm 118:19-29
Lesson 2	Romans 8:6-11	Philippians 2:5-11	Philippians 2:5-11
Gospel	John 11:(1-16), 17-45	Matthew 26:14–27:66 *or* Matthew 27:11-54	Matthew 21:1-11
B. Lesson 1	Jeremiah 31:31-34 Psalm 51:10-17	Same as A Psalm 31:9-16	Same as A Psalm 118:19-29
Lesson 2	Hebrews 5:7-10	Same as A	Same as A
Gospel	John 12:20-33	Mark 14:1–15:47 *or* Mark 15:1-39	Mark 11:1-11 *or* John 12:12-16
C. Lesson 1	Isaiah 43:16-21 Psalm 126	Same as A Psalm 31:9-16	Same as A Psalm 118:19-29
Lesson 2	Philippians 3:8-14	Same as A	Same as A
Gospel	John 12:1-8	Luke 22:14–23:56 *or* Luke 23:1-49	Luke 19:28-40

*These readings are provided for the liturgy or procession of palms for churches which have not had the tradition of readings-and-procession and also for an early "said" service in the Episcopal tradition.

HOLY WEEK

		Monday	Tuesday	Wednesday	Holy Thursday*	Good Friday
A.	Lesson 1	Isaiah 42:1-9 Psalm 36:5-10	Isaiah 49:1-7 Psalm 71:1-12	Isaiah 50:4-9a Psalm 70	Exodus 12:1-14 Psalm 116:12-19**	Isaiah 52:13–53:12 Psalm 22:1-18
	Lesson 2	Hebrews 9:11-15	I Corinthians 1:18-31	Hebrews 12:1-3	I Corinthians 11:23-26	Hebrews 4:14-16; 5:7-9
	Gospel	John 12:1-11	John 12:20-36	John 13:21-30	John 13:1-15	John 18:1–19:42 *or* John 19:17-30
B.	Lesson 1				Exodus 24:3-8 Psalm 116:12-19	
	Lesson 2				I Corinthians 10:16-17	
	Gospel				Mark 14:12-26	
C.	Lesson 1				Jeremiah 31:31-34 Psalm 116:12-19	
	Lesson 2				Hebrews 10:16-25	
	Gospel				Luke 22:7-20	

*For those who want the feet washing emphasis every year, ''A'' readings are used each year.

**Psalm 116 is used at the Lord's Supper on Holy Thursday. Psalm 89:20-21, 24, 26 is used at the ''chrism'' service.

EASTER VIGIL*

Old Testament Readings and Psalms (A, B, C)

Genesis 1:1–2:2   Isaiah 55:1-11
  Psalm 33   Isaiah 12:2-6
Genesis 7:1-5, 11-18; 8:6-18; 9:8-13   Baruch 3:9-15, 32–4:4
  Psalm 46   Psalm 19
Genesis 22:1-18   Ezekiel 36:24-28
  Psalm 16   Psalm 42
Exodus 14:10–15:1   Ezekiel 37:1-14
  Exodus 15:1-6, 11-13, 17-18   Psalm 143
Isaiah 54:5-14   Zephaniah 3:14-20
  Psalm 30   Psalm 98

Second Reading (A, B, C)
Romans 6:3-11
Psalm 114

Gospel
A. Matthew 28:1-10
B. Mark 16:1-8
C. Luke 24:1-12

*This selection of readings and psalms is provided for the Easter Vigil. A minimum of three readings from the Old Testament should be used, and this should always include Exodus 14.

	Easter* **	Second Sunday of Easter	Third Sunday of Easter	Fourth Sunday of Easter	Fifth Sunday of Easter
A. Lesson 1	Acts 10:34-43 / or / Jeremiah 31:1-6 / Psalm 118:14-24	Acts 2:14a, 22-32 / Psalm 16:5-11	Acts 2:14a, 36-41 / Psalm 116:12-19	Acts 2:42-47 / Psalm 23	Acts 7:55-60 / Psalm 31:1-8
Lesson 2	Colossians 3:1-4 / or / Acts 10:34-43	I Peter 1:3-9	I Peter 1:17-23	I Peter 2:19-25	I Peter 2:2-10
Gospel	John 20:1-18 / or / Matthew 28:1-10	John 20:19-31	Luke 24:13-35	John 10:1-10	John 14:1-14
B. Lesson 1	Acts 10:34-43 / or / Isaiah 25:6-9 / Psalm 118:14-24	Acts 4:32-35 / Psalm 133	Acts 3:12-19 / Psalm 4	Acts 4:8-12 / Psalm 23	Acts 8:26-40 / Psalm 22:25-31
Lesson 2	I Corinthians 15:1-11 / or / Acts 10:34-43	I John 1:1—2:2	I John 3:1-7	I John 3:18-24	I John 4:7-12
Gospel	John 20:1-18 / or / Mark 16:1-8	John 20:19-31	Luke 24:35-48	John 10:11-18	John 15:1-8

*See next page for Easter Evening.

**If the Old Testament passage is chosen for the first reading, the Acts passage is used as the second reading in order to initiate the sequential reading of Acts during the fifty days of Easter.

		Easter*	Second Sunday of Easter	Third Sunday of Easter	Fourth Sunday of Easter	Fifth Sunday of Easter
C.	Lesson 1	Acts 10:34-43 _or_ Isaiah 65:17-25 Psalm 118:14-24	Acts 5:27-32 Psalm 2	Acts 9:1-20 Psalm 30:4-12	Acts 13:15-16, 26-33 Psalm 23	Acts 14:8-18 Psalm 145:13b-21
	Lesson 2	I Corinthians 15:19-26 _or_ Acts 10:34-43	Revelation 1:4-8	Revelation 5:11-14	Revelation 7:9-17	Revelation 21:1-6
	Gospel	John 20:1-18 _or_ Luke 24:1-12	John 20:19-31	John 21:1-19 _or_ John 21:15-19	John 10:22-30	John 13:31-35

Easter Evening*

		Easter Evening*
A.	Lesson 1	Acts 5:29-32 _or_ Daniel 12:1-3 Psalm 150
	Lesson 2	I Corinthians 5:6-8 _or_ Acts 5:29-32
	Gospel	Luke 24:13-49

*If the first reading is from the Old Testament, the reading from Acts should be second.

	Sixth Sunday of Easter	Ascension*	Seventh Sunday of Easter	Pentecost**	Trinity Sunday
A. Lesson 1	Acts 17:22-31 Psalm 66:8-20	Acts 1:1-11 Psalm 47	Acts 1:6-14 Psalm 68:1-10	Acts 2:1-21 *or* Isaiah 44:1-8 Psalm 104:24-34	Deuteronomy 4:32-40 Psalm 33:1-12
Lesson 2	I Peter 3:13-22	Ephesians 1:15-23	I Peter 4:12-14; 5:6-11	I Corinthians 12:3b-13 *or* Acts 2:1-21	II Corinthians 13:5-14
Gospel	John 14:15-21	Luke 24:46-53 *or* Mark 16:9-16, 19-20	John 17:1-11	John 20:19-23 *or* John 7:37-39	Matthew 28:16-20
B. Lesson 1	Acts 10:44-48 Psalm 98	Psalm 47	Acts 1:15-17, 21-26 Psalm 1	Acts 2:1-21 *or* Ezekiel 37:1-14 Psalm 104:24-34	Isaiah 6:1-8 Psalm 29
Lesson 2	I John 5:1-6		I John 5:9-13	Romans 8:22-27 *or* Acts 2:1-21	Romans 8:12-17
Gospel	John 15:9-17		John 17:11b-19	John 15:26-27; 16:4b-15	John 3:1-17

*Or on Seventh Sunday of Easter.

**If the Old Testament passage is chosen for the first reading, the Acts passage is used as the second reading.

	Sixth Sunday of Easter	Ascension*	Seventh Sunday of Easter	Pentecost**	Trinity Sunday
C. Lesson 1	Acts 15:1-2, 22-29 Psalm 67	Psalm 47	Acts 16:16-34 Psalm 97	Acts 2:1-21 *or* Genesis 11:1-9 Psalm 104:24-34	Proverbs 8:22-31 Psalm 8
Lesson 2	Revelation 21:10, 22-27		Revelation 22:12-14, 16-17, 20	Romans 8:14-17 *or* Acts 2:1-21	Romans 5:1-5
Gospel	John 14:23-29		John 17:20-26	John 14:8-17, 25-27	John 16:12-15

*Or on Seventh Sunday of Easter.

**If the Old Testament passage is chosen for the first reading, the Acts passage is used as the second reading.

	Proper 4* Sunday between May 29 and June 4 inclusive (if after Trinity Sunday)	Proper 5 Sunday between June 5 and 11 inclusive (if after Trinity Sunday)	Proper 6 Sunday between June 12 and 18 inclusive (if after Trinity Sunday)	Proper 7 Sunday between June 19 and 25 inclusive (if after Trinity Sunday)	Proper 8 Sunday between June 26 and July 2 inclusive
A. Lesson 1	Genesis 12:1-9 Psalm 33:12-22	Genesis 22:1-18 Psalm 13	Genesis 25:19-34 Psalm 46	Genesis 28:10-17 Psalm 91:1-10	Genesis 32:22-32 Psalm 17:1-7, 15
Lesson 2	Romans 3:21-28	Romans 4:13-18	Romans 5:6-11	Romans 5:12-19	Romans 6:3-11
Gospel	Matthew 7:21-29	Matthew 9:9-13	Matthew 9:35–10:8	Matthew 10:24-33	Matthew 10:34-42
B. Lesson 1	I Samuel 16:1-13 Psalm 20	I Samuel 16:14-23 Psalm 57	II Samuel 1:1, 17-27 Psalm 46	II Samuel 5:1-12 Psalm 48	II Samuel 6:1-15 Psalm 24
Lesson 2	II Corinthians 4:5-12	II Corinthians 4:13–5:1	II Corinthians 5:6-10, 14-17	II Corinthians 5:18–6:2	II Corinthians 8:7-15
Gospel	Mark 2:23–3:6	Mark 3:20-35	Mark 4:26-34	Mark 4:35-41	Mark 5:21-43
C. Lesson 1	I Kings 8:22-23, 41-43 Psalm 100	I Kings 17:17-24 Psalm 113	I Kings 19:1-8 Psalm 42	I Kings 19:9-14 Psalm 43	I Kings 19:15-21 Psalm 44:1-8
Lesson 2	Galatians 1:1-10	Galatians 1:11-24	Galatians 2:15-21	Galatians 3:23-29	Galatians 5:1, 13-25
Gospel	Luke 7:1-10	Luke 7:11-17	Luke 7:36–8:3	Luke 9:18-24	Luke 9:51-62

*If the Sunday between May 24 and 28 inclusive follows Trinity Sunday, use Eighth Sunday After Epiphany on that day.

	Proper 9 Sunday between July 3 and 9 inclusive	Proper 10 Sunday between July 10 and 16 inclusive	Proper 11 Sunday between July 17 and 23 inclusive	Proper 12 Sunday between July 24 and 30 inclusive	Proper 13 Sunday between July 31 and Aug. 6 inclusive
A. Lesson 1	Exodus 1:6-14, 22–2:10 Psalm 124	Exodus 2:11-22 Psalm 69:6-15	Exodus 3:1-12 Psalm 103:1-13	Exodus 3:13-20 Psalm 105:1-11	Exodus 12:1-14 Psalm 143:1-10
Lesson 2	Romans 7:14-25a	Romans 8:9-17	Romans 8:18-25	Romans 8:26-30	Romans 8:31-39
Gospel	Matthew 11:25-30	Matthew 13:1-9, 18-23	Matthew 13:24-30, 36-43	Matthew 13:44-52	Matthew 14:13-21
B. Lesson 1	II Samuel 7:1-17 Psalm 89:20-37	II Samuel 7:18-29 Psalm 132:11-18	II Samuel 11:1-15 Psalm 53	II Samuel 12:1-14 Psalm 32	II Samuel 12:15b-24 Psalm 34:11-22
Lesson 2	II Corinthians 12:1-10	Ephesians 1:1-10	Ephesians 2:11-22	Ephesians 3:14-21	Ephesians 4:1-6
Gospel	Mark 6:1-6	Mark 6:7-13	Mark 6:30-34	John 6:1-15	John 6:24-35
C. Lesson 1	I Kings 21:1-3, 17-21 Psalm 5:1-8	II Kings 2:1, 6-14 Psalm 139:1-12	II Kings 4:8-17 Psalm 139:13-18	II Kings 5:1-15ab ("... in Israel") Psalm 21:1-7	II Kings 13:14-20a Psalm 28
Lesson 2	Galatians 6:7-18	Colossians 1:1-14	Colossians 1:21-29	Colossians 2:6-15	Colossians 3:1-11
Gospel	Luke 10:1-12, 17-20	Luke 10:25-37	Luke 10:38-42	Luke 11:1-13	Luke 12:13-21

		Proper 14 Sunday between August 7 and 13 inclusive	Proper 15 Sunday between August 14 and 20 inclusive	Proper 16 Sunday between August 21 and 27 inclusive	Proper 17 Sunday between August 28 and Sept. 3 inclusive	Proper 18 Sunday between September 4 and 10 inclusive
A.	Lesson 1	Exodus 14:19-31 Psalm 106:4-12	Exodus 16:2-15 Psalm 78:1-3, 10-20	Exodus 17:1-7 Psalm 95	Exodus 19:1-9 Psalm 114	Exodus 19:16-24 Psalm 115:1-11
	Lesson 2	Romans 9:1-5	Romans 11:13-16, 29-32	Romans 11:33-36	Romans 12:1-13	Romans 13:1-10
	Gospel	Matthew 14:22-33	Matthew 15:21-28	Matthew 16:13-20	Matthew 16:21-28	Matthew 18:15-20
B.	Lesson 1	II Samuel 18:1, 5, 9-15 Psalm 143:1-8	II Samuel 18:24-33 Psalm 102:1-12	II Samuel 23:1-7 Psalm 67	I Kings 2:1-4, 10-12 Psalm 121	Ecclesiasticus 5:8-15 or Proverbs 2:1-8 Psalm 119:129-136
	Lesson 2	Ephesians 4:25—5:2	Ephesians 5:15-20	Ephesians 5:21-33	Ephesians 6:10-20	James 1:17-27
	Gospel	John 6:35, 41-51	John 6:51-58	John 6:55-69	Mark 7:1-8, 14-15, 21-23	Mark 7:31-37
C.	Lesson 1	Jeremiah 18:1-11 Psalm 14	Jeremiah 20:7-13 Psalm 10:12-18	Jeremiah 28:1-9 Psalm 84	Ezekiel 18:1-9, 25-29 Psalm 15	Ezekiel 33:1-11 Psalm 94:12-22
	Lesson 2	Hebrews 11:1-3, 8-19	Hebrews 12:1-2, 12-17	Hebrews 12:18-29	Hebrews 13:1-8	Philemon 1-20
	Gospel	Luke 12:32-40	Luke 12:49-56	Luke 13:22-30	Luke 14:1, 7-14	Luke 14:25-33

		Proper 19 Sunday between September 11 and 17 inclusive	Proper 20 Sunday between September 18 and 24 inclusive	Proper 21 Sunday between Sept. 25 and Oct. 1 inclusive	Proper 22 Sunday between October 2 and 8 inclusive	Proper 23 Sunday between October 9 and 15 inclusive
A.	Lesson 1	Exodus 20:1-20 Psalm 19:7-14	Exodus 32:1-14 Psalm 106:7-8, 19-23	Exodus 33:12-23 Psalm 99	Numbers 27:12-23 Psalm 81:1-10	Deuteronomy 34:1-12 Psalm 135:1-14
	Lesson 2	Romans 14:5-12	Philippians 1:21-27	Philippians 2:1-13	Philippians 3:12-21	Philippians 4:1-9
	Gospel	Matthew 18:21-35	Matthew 20:1-16	Matthew 21:28-32	Matthew 21:33-43	Matthew 22:1-14
B.	Lesson 1	Proverbs 22:1-2, 8-9 Psalm 125	Job 28:20-28 Psalm 27:1-6	Job 42:1-6 Psalm 27:7-14	Genesis 2:18-24 Psalm 128	Genesis 3:8-19 Psalm 90:1-12
	Lesson 2	James 2:1-5, 8-10, 14-17	James 3:13-18	James 4:13-17; 5:7-11	Hebrews 1:1-4; 2:9-11	Hebrews 4:1-3, 9-13
	Gospel	Mark 8:27-38	Mark 9:30-37	Mark 9:38-50	Mark 10:2-16	Mark 10:17-30
C.	Lesson 1	Hosea 4:1-3, 5:15—6:6 Psalm 77:11-20	Hosea 11:1-11 Psalm 107:1-9	Joel 2:23-30 Psalm 107:1, 33-43	Amos 5:6-7, 10-15 Psalm 101	Micah 1:2; 2:1-10 Psalm 26
	Lesson 2	I Timothy 1:12-17	I Timothy 2:1-7	I Timothy 6:6-19	II Timothy 1:1-14	II Timothy 2:8-15
	Gospel	Luke 15:1-10	Luke 16:1-13	Luke 16:19-31	Luke 17:5-10	Luke 17:11-19

		Proper 24 Sunday between October 16 and 22 inclusive	Proper 25 Sunday between October 23 and 29 inclusive	Proper 26 Sunday between October 30 and Nov. 5 inclusive	Proper 27 Sunday between November 6 and 12 inclusive	Proper 28 Sunday between November 13 and 19 inclusive
A.	Lesson 1	Ruth 1:1-19a Psalm 146	Ruth 2:1-13 Psalm 128	Ruth 4:7-17 Psalm 127	Amos 5:18-24 Psalm 50:7-15	Zephaniah 1:7, 12-18 Psalm 76
	Lesson 2	I Thessalonians 1:1-10	I Thessalonians 2:1-8	I Thessalonians 2:9-13, 17-20	I Thessalonians 4:13-18	I Thessalonians 5:1-11
	Gospel	Matthew 22:15-22	Matthew 22:34-46	Matthew 23:1-12	Matthew 25:1-13	Matthew 25:14-30
B.	Lesson 1	Isaiah 53:7-12 Psalm 35:17-28	Jeremiah 31:7-9 Psalm 126	Deuteronomy 6:1-9 Psalm 119:33-48	I Kings 17:8-16 Psalm 146	Daniel 7:9-14 Psalm 145:8-13
	Lesson 2	Hebrews 4:14-16	Hebrews 5:1-6	Hebrews 7:23-28	Hebrews 9:24-28	Hebrews 10:11-18
	Gospel	Mark 10:35-45	Mark 10:46-52	Mark 12:28-34	Mark 12:38-44	Mark 13:24-32
C.	Lesson 1	Habakkuk 1:1-3; 2:1-4	Zephaniah 3:1-9	Haggai 2:1-9	Zechariah 7:1-10	Malachi 4:1-6 (3:19-24 in Hebrews)
		Psalm 119:137-144	Psalm 3	Psalm 65:1-8	Psalm 9:11-20	Psalm 82
	Lesson 2	II Timothy 3:14-4:5	II Timothy 4:6-8, 16-18	II Thessalonians 1:5-12	II Thessalonians 2:13-3:5	II Thessalonians 3:6-13
	Gospel	Luke 18:1-8	Luke 18:9-14	Luke 19:1-10	Luke 20:27-38	Luke 21:5-19

	Proper 29 (Christ the King) Sunday between November 20 and 26 inclusive	All Saints, November 1*	Thanksgiving Day**
A. Lesson 1	Ezekiel 34:11-16, 20-24 Psalm 23	Revelation 7:9-17 Psalm 34:1-10	Deuteronomy 8:7-18 Psalm 65
Lesson 2	I Corinthians 15:20-28	I John 3:1-3	II Corinthians 9:6-15
Gospel	Matthew 25:31-46	Matthew 5:1-12	Luke 17:11-19
B. Lesson 1	Jeremiah 23:1-6 Psalm 93	Revelation 21:1-6a Psalm 24:1-6	Joel 2:21-27 Psalm 126
Lesson 2	Revelation 1:4b-8	Colossians 1:9-14	I Timothy 2:1-7
Gospel	John 18:33-37	John 11:32-44	Matthew 6:25-33
C. Lesson 1	II Samuel 5:1-5 Psalm 95	Daniel 7:1-3, 15-18 Psalm 149	Deuteronomy 26:1-11 Psalm 100
Lesson 2	Colossians 1:11-20	Ephesians 1:11-23	Philippians 4:4-9
Gospel	John 12:9-19	Luke 6:20-36	John 6:25-35

*Or on first Sunday in November.
**Readings *ad libitum*, not tied to A, B, or C.

	Annunciation March 25	Visitation May 31	Presentation February 2	Holy Cross September 14
A. Lesson 1	Isaiah 7:10-14 Psalm 45 or 40:6-10	I Samuel 2:1-10 Psalm 113	Malachi 3:1-4 Psalm 84 or 24:7-10	Numbers 21:4b-9 Psalm 98:1-5 or 78:1-2, 34-38
Lesson 2	Hebrews 10:4-10	Romans 12:9-16b	Hebrews 2:14-18	I Corinthians 1:18-24
Gospel	Luke 1:26-38	Luke 1:39-57	Luke 2:22-40	John 3:13-17

Titles of Seasons, Sundays, and Special Days

Advent Season

First Sunday of Advent................The Sunday occurring November 27 to December 3
Second Sunday of Advent................The Sunday occurring December 4 to December 10
Third Sunday of Advent................The Sunday occurring December 11 to December 17
Fourth Sunday of Advent................The Sunday occurring December 18 to December 24

Christmas Season

Christmas Eve/Day................December 24/25
First Sunday After Christmas................The Sunday occurring December 26 to January 1
New Year's Eve/Day................December 31 to January 1
Second Sunday After Christmas................The Sunday occurring January 2 to January 5

Epiphany Season

Epiphany................January 6 or first Sunday in January
First Sunday After Epiphany (Baptism of the Lord)................The Sunday occurring January 7 to January 13
Second Sunday After Epiphany................The Sunday occurring January 14 to January 20
Third Sunday After Epiphany................The Sunday occurring January 21 to January 27
Fourth Sunday After Epiphany*................The Sunday occurring January 28 to February 3
Fifth Sunday After Epiphany*................The Sunday occurring February 4 to February 10
Sixth Sunday After Epiphany (Proper 1)*................The Sunday occurring February 11 to February 17
Seventh Sunday After Epiphany (Proper 2)*................The Sunday occurring February 18 to February 24
Eighth Sunday After Epiphany (Proper 3)*................The Sunday occurring February 25 to February 29
Last Sunday After Epiphany (Transfiguration Sunday)

*Except when this Sunday is the Last Sunday After Epiphany.

Lenten Season

Ash Wednesday: Seventh
   Wednesday Before Easter
First Sunday of Lent
Second Sunday of Lent
Third Sunday of Lent
Fourth Sunday of Lent
Fifth Sunday of Lent

Holy Week

Passion/Palm Sunday
Monday in Holy Week
Tuesday in Holy Week
Wednesday in Holy Week
Holy Thursday
Good Friday
(Holy Saturday)

Easter Season

Easter Vigil
Easter
Easter Evening
Second Sunday of Easter
Third Sunday of Easter
Fourth Sunday of Easter
Fifth Sunday of Easter
Sixth Sunday of Easter
Ascension (fortieth day, sixth Thursday of Easter)
Seventh Sunday of Easter
Pentecost

Season After Pentecost

Trinity Sunday (First Sunday After Pentecost)
Propers 4–28 (See note below.)
Proper 29, Christ the King: the Sunday occurring
   November 20 to 26

Special Days

Some special days observed by many churches are included in the table, with appropriate readings and psalms.

NOTE: Easter is a movable feast, and can occur as early as March 22 and as late as April 25. When Easter is early, it encroaches on the Sundays after Epiphany, reducing their number, as necessary, from as many as nine to as few as four. In similar fashion the date of Easter determines the number of Sunday Propers after Pentecost. When Easter is as early as March 22, the numbered Proper for the Sunday following Trinity Sunday is Proper 3.